STO

It's All Arranged

FIFTEEN HOURS IN A PSYCHIATRIST'S LIFE

It's All Arranged

FIFTEEN HOURS
IN A PSYCHIATRIST'S LIFE

A. H. Chapman, MD

G. P. Putnam's Sons
New York

SBN 399-11428-9
Library of Congress Catalog Card Number: 74-16584

PRINTED IN THE UNITED STATES OF AMERICA

To the memory of
DANIEL CADY DARROW,
late professor of pediatrics,
Yale University School of Medicine and
the University of Kansas School of Medicine,
and for
JEFFREY CRAIG CHAPMAN

Preface

THE time of this book is the indefinite present.
It covers one day in my practice of psychiatry; there have
been thousands of such days. The precise day is not
important; to preserve the anonymity of patients, it is not
specified. From one year to the next, from one generation to
the next, the agony and perplexity of patients remain
largely the same. The trimmings vary and the jargon alters a
little, but the basic emotional problems of people continue
unchanged. Sigmund Freud was in the private practice of
psychiatry in Vienna for more than fifty years and never
dated a case report; it is bf no consequence, since his cases
remain as fresh and relevant to the problems of modern
patients as when he wrote them in the first two decades of
this century. The same is true of the cases of Adolf Meyer,
Harry Stack Sullivan, Frieda Fromm-Reichmann, and the
many other clinicians who built the structure of modern
psychiatry.

Harry Stack Sullivan, now generally recognized as the
most original and important American-born psychiatrist,
had a dictum: "We are all much more simply human than
otherwise." By this he meant, among other things, that in
the problems of each patient we see a little of ourselves
—perhaps distorted and exaggerated, but nevertheless more
akin to our lives than we often care to confess. In learning
more about those whom we call sick, we learn a good deal
about those whom we call healthy.

A. H. C.

"Doctor," said Ballow, ". . . the ancients endeavoured to make physic a science, and failed; and the moderns to make it a trade, and have succeeded."

—Sir John Hawkins, *Life of Samuel Johnson*

1

ON Monday mornings I give electroshock treatments at Mt. Sinai, a large hospital in midtown Kansas City, and I arrive on the ward at 7:00. It is still dark, and the lights of the nurses' station make a bright glare from which the grayness spreads out.

Tom Evans is there behind the long desk with his fifteen metal-cased patients' charts piled in front of him. He looks up as I lean over the counter to pick up my four charts.

"Good morning, Harry."

"Good morning, Tom."

"Cold this morning," he says, "but I got in before the snow started to fall."

"Good for you."

Lucky Tom. He always has a smooth ten-second conversational to-and-fro for everyone. For the doctors, the nurses, the aides, the patients, and for anybody who happens to be in the elevator. A very nice guy.

He makes more money than I like to think about. Fifteen charts on the psychiatric ward at Mt. Sinai, a few consultations on the medical floors upstairs, more charts at St. Catharine's, and his office practice. And he collects it all. He feels that patients "should be responsible for their obligations." You can't argue with that.

Tom Evans reads his charts and twiddles his cigarette between his dainty fingers with their well-manicured nails. He sucks on his cigarettes; sometimes I think of somebody sucking a penis when Tom Evans smokes.

Tom Evans bothers me. There are lots of reasons why Tom Evans bothers me. He makes four or five times as much money as I do, though I do well enough for myself. He's a lousy psychiatrist. I know. I've seen enough of his former patients in consultation and I covered his practice once when he went to Acapulco for three weeks.

How does a lousy psychiatrist make all that money, have all those patients, and keep that constant stream of consultations flowing into his hands? That puzzled me for a long time when I first went into practice, but in time I figured it out. He does what the referring doctors want, and he knows what the patients and their relatives will tolerate.

When called to see a patient on a medical floor, Tom Evans knows what the referring doctor wants. He has talked to him briefly on the phone and he reads the consultation request shrewdly. Sometimes he doesn't even have to do that, if he knows the doctor well enough. He knows that when Dr. Brown calls in a psychiatrist, it's because he's sick of the patient and wants to get rid of him. Tom Evans gets rid of him. He knows that Dr. Jones thinks psychotherapy is bunk and only electroshock treatment ever helps anybody. That patient gets shock. Tom Evans knows that Dr. Smith usually wants a little chitchat and the latest tranquilizers for his referrals. Tom Evans obliges.

Tom knows how to sort the patients out, both in the hospital and in his office. Patients who are unlikely to pay their bills are given vague referrals to two or three public facilities that they are unlikely to get into. If they come back, his secretary handles them. However, patients who have money are given diagnoses, and treatments are recommended. If the patient cries or looks as if he is about to cry, he has a depression. An antidepressant medication is prescribed, along with a little supportive conversation; if he isn't well in thirty days or if his relatives call too much on the telephone, he is sent to the hospital for shock treatments. If a patient is shy and acts a little strange, he has schizophrenia; for that, an antipsychotic medication and psychotherapy (ten-minute sessions) are given. If he doesn't get well or go away, or if his relatives are unhappy about what's going on, the patient is put in the hospital and the same medication and ten-minute sessions continue. If the patient is nasty and troublesome, he has a "hostile, antisocial personality and would not cooperate in psychotherapy." That gets rid of him. Also, since he wouldn't cooperate in treatment, it's his own fault that he didn't get well. That gets the referring doctor off the hook, and it also gets Tom Evans off the hook.

It took me two to three years to figure all this out. Tom Evans is a very successful psychiatrist because he is very good at getting doctors off hooks.

The nurses come out of their cubbyhole. The aides come behind them. They have been changing shifts. The shifts change at 7 A.M., 3 P.M., and 11 P.M. Each time the nurses huddle as the outgoing crew rattles through the list of patients, and the new shift listens. The aides stand there. "Mrs. Green had a poor night, needed a repeat on her sedation." "Miss Rosen banged on the door of the seclusion room until she had a hypo." "Mr. Marden was quiet." There are thirty-seven more patients to run through.

Miss Moore, bright and fresh from Springfield in the Ozarks, smiles at Dr. Evans and me. Pretty little Miss Moore likes Kansas City and being a psychiatric nurse. She won't be a psychiatric nurse long, however. Someone will marry her. I hope she gets a good husband. She's a nice kid.

11

"Miss Moore, I have only two shock treatments and Dr. Evans has fifteen."

"Eight," he corrects me. He resents the inference that he gives shock to everybody.

"Four times more than I do," I return cheerfully. This cuts two ways. It needles Dr. Evans by implying that I fry fewer brains than he does, and it also prepares the way for my next move.

"Let's give my two, and by the time Dr. Evans gets through reading his charts, the shock room will be ready for him." Tom Evans' name is on the shock schedule to give his treatments before I do, and I'm not supposed to cut in ahead of him. But I don't want to sit around while Tom gives eight electroshock treatments.

Pretty Miss Moore and I walk through the door of the nurses' station. Tom Evans frowns slightly, but he has been outmaneuvered. He returns to his charts.

"Miss Moore, I'll get Mr. Rattner while you get the shock room ready." She trots off. It's nice to watch Miss Moore when she trots off, but I don't have time this morning.

Mr. Rattner is sitting on the edge of his bed.

"Doctor, my bowels haven't—"

I cut him short and tell him that it's time for his treatment. I hustle him out into the hall and into the shock room. I really should sit and listen to him for a few minutes, but I can't tell him that Dr. Thomas R. Evans has eight electroshock treatments and that I outmaneuvered him, and so Dr. Evans can't be kept waiting.

The aide takes Mr. Rattner into the adjoining toilet to urinate. It's routine. If not, the patient may wet his clothing during the slight initial muscular spasm of the shock treatment.

I glance at the tray beside the shock table. Everything is there. Miss Moore smiles. She ought to be smiling at

12

somebody over a breakfast table at this time of the morning. In another year or two she probably will be.

Mr. Rattner and the aide emerge from the toilet. Mr. Rattner is still buttoning his fly. He is a little embarrassed by this, but the aide pushes Mr. Rattner along; he knows that Dr. Evans will soon be upon us and that his nasty little words will slash us if he is kept waiting.

"Up on the table," I say cheerily, and the aide and I halfway hoist him onto it. The aide slips his shoes off.

"My wife was here yesterday and she asked if I might—"

I cut him off by saying that we can talk about that after the treatment. A lie. He won't be fully alert for an hour or more after the treatment, and I shall have left the ward by then.

"Let's lie down, Mr. Rattner," says Miss Moore. The aide slips a small, firm pillow under his lower back and Miss Moore adjusts another one under his neck, thrusting his chin upward as he reclines.

She removes his glasses and puts them on the tray.

"Any dentures?"

A small bridge comes out and is placed beside the glasses. All easily breakable things are removed before the treatment begins. The aide loosens his belt and slips a third, oblong pillow under his knees as Miss Moore rolls up his left shirt sleeve and quickly snaps a narrow rubber tube around his upper arm.

Mr. Rattner has good veins. I reach out my hand to Miss Moore and she gives me a small bit of alcohol-soaked cotton that I quickly rub over the bulging veins on his fish-belly white underarm. I toss the cotton into a nearby plastic bucket and stretch my hand out for the syringe of barbiturate.

"Just a pinprick, a mosquito bite," and I jab the needle into Mr. Rattner's vein. I pull back slightly on the bolt and

13

dark blood spurts into the clear saline with the barbiturate in it. I am in the vein. I snap the rubber tourniquet off his arm and slowly begin to inject. I glance at my wristwatch.

In sixty seconds ten cubic centimeters of barbiturate solution have been injected, and Mr. Rattner is asleep. I grasp the butt of the needle firmly between the thumb and forefinger of my left hand and rotate the syringe slightly with my right hand. It comes loose, leaving the needle in the vein. I hold the blood-tinged syringe out to Miss Moore, who takes it and places another syringe with thirty units of succinylcholine into my hand. I carefully insert this syringe into the needle and pull back on the bolt of the syringe. A jet of blood assures me that I am still in the vein.

I inject the succinylcholine rapidly, remove the needle and syringe, and apply a fluff of dry cotton to the injection site.

Succinylcholine paralyzes muscles for two to three minutes. It greatly softens the force of the convulsive muscular movements of electroshock. It has made shock treatment a fairly harmless procedure.

Before they invented succinylcholine, electroshock treatment was ghastly. The patients had violent muscular contractions of the entire body for about forty seconds, and three percent of the patients or more had fractures. In my military service during the Korean War I gave twenty-five of them each morning three days a week. We ran them in and out on wheeled treatment tables. We had a resident orthopedist to take care of the fractures.

I watch Mr. Rattner carefully. After forty-five seconds his eyelids twitch and his lips quiver slightly. The succinylocholine has taken effect. I move quickly to the head of the table. One aide steadies Mr. Rattner's knees and another leans across his chest and pins his arms down to the table. Miss Moore inserts a rubber gag, pierced by an airway tube,

14

into his mouth to keep him from biting his lips during the treatment. She steadies his chin.

During this ten-second period I have flicked on the shock machine. Its red button lights up. A practical nurse sponges off small spots on Mr. Rattner's temples as Miss Moore watches her; the practical nurse puts a slight film of electrode paste on each of two felt-covered electrodes and then places them on his temples. We are about to send a ninety-volt current through his head for a few seconds.

"Okay?"

"Okay," Miss Moore replies.

I turn a switch, build up the current for five seconds, level it off for five seconds more, and flick off the machine.

Mr. Rattner stiffens out slightly for ten seconds, and then his limbs ripple gently for another thirty seconds. Bless the Swiss chemists, or whoever it was who discovered succinylcholine!

The treatment is over. However, the succinylcholine will take another minute or two to wear off, and during that time we must keep Mr. Rattner breathing, since his respiratory muscles are paralyzed. Miss Moore hands me the positive-pressure hand respirator. I clamp the black rubber mask tightly over his nose and mouth and pump the attached rubber bag every three seconds with my free hand. His chest expands and contracts regularly as I pump air in and out of him.

"How's your new boyfriend, Miss Moore?"

She laughs. The aides grin.

"Psychologists make bad husbands. They usually beat their wives."

More laughter.

"I'm not fooling. I read an article that proves it statistically."

"Mr. Temple is a pretty big fellow, too," a black aide

says. Mr. Temple is a graduate student in psychology who works as a part-time aide on weekends and dates Miss Moore. He is tall and wiry, with thick glasses and unruly hair. Many girls wouldn't look at him twice, but to Miss Moore, fresh from the Ozarks, a PhD student in psychology looks very good.

Mr. Rattner begins to push back against the pressure of my hand on the respirator bag. He is now breathing on his own.

"Okay, Montgomery." The two black aides take over. They wheel up a stretcher, lift him onto it, strap him down, and take him sleeping back to his room.

Miss Moore gets the medication tray ready for the next patient and the practical nurse smoothes out the electroshock-treatment table as I go to room 117 to get Miss Draper.

Miss Draper is a very different kind of case from Mr. Rattner. Mr. Rattner is a poor Jew who works as an attendant in a downtown parking lot. Every five years or so he goes into a severe depression and stops working. His wife brings him to me. I hospitalize him for three weeks, give him five or six electroshock treatments, and he's as good as new. When he gets well, he becomes a chipper little man who whistles, jokes, and clowns with the customers; everyone calls him Sammy. He has well-to-do relatives who never come to see him in the hospital or at any other time apparently. His wife, who has hemorrhoids and varicose veins, complains about it.

I feel sorry for the Rattners and charge them only a few dollars more than Blue Shield pays. I should charge them more. If a psychiatrist doesn't, word gets around and pretty soon he has too many poor Jews in his practice. Tom Evans would know how to get rid of them. There are greener pastures.

16

Miss Draper is a seventeen-year-old girl in her third schizophrenic illness. Her first one occurred when she was fifteen. With an antipsychotic medication and some supportive psychotherapy she got well. But she didn't stay well. Eight months later she again began to complain that the kids at high school were whispering that she was a homosexual, and she said that the water tasted strange because someone had put "dope" in it. This time she had another antipsychotic medication, supportive counseling, and shock therapy, and her illness lasted longer. But she recovered. Then, after a year, it all came back again.

Her parents are scared lower-middle-class people; her father does office work in a grain brokerage firm. Their hospitalization insurance is about to run out. I have told them that "It may take a while this time" and have urged them to transfer her to a municipal or state psychiatric hospital. They are stalling, hoping and praying for a recovery that is improbable. She may get well, but it will take months, and even then her hold on reality may be weak. In a few days I must call her parents in and firmly insist that she be transferred. Her mother will cry and her father will stare helplessly at me. I will give them the names of the admission social workers at the municipal psychiatric receiving center and the nearest state hospital.

Miss Draper is not to be found. I look for a female aide to search the women's lavatory for her. Dr. Thomas Evans walks onto the floor. He has finished reading his charts and is ready to consume a little electricity.

I find a female aide who gets Miss Draper from the women's lavatory. Miss Draper does not want her treatment. She is afraid of it. I should talk with her, but I don't have time. Dr. Thomas Evans, who has fifteen patients in this hospital alone, is pushing me.

One of the black male aides comes up. He starts a gentle

stream of chatter, and by steadying one arm and getting a practical nurse to hold the other, he steers Miss Draper toward the treatment room.

Miss Draper is on the table. Her eyes flit wildly from one of us to the other. God only knows what voices are shrieking in her ears and what weird thoughts are running through her mind as we prepare to stick a needle into her arm and send a charge of electricity through her head.

I jab her and pull back on the bolt of the syringe. No blood. I am not in the vein. I jab her three more times.

"Let's try the other arm."

Miss Moore loosens the tourniquet and puts it on the other arm. I massage the forearm upward from the wrist on its undersurface to distend any small veins that hold promise of receiving a needle. I slowly stab her again, and the needle slides along the side of a vein. I give it a short push and it enters. I pull back on the bolt of the syringe and blood spurts into it. I relax a little, Miss Moore releases the tourniquet, and I begin to inject the barbiturate.

The door to the room opens and Dr. Evans comes in.

"Your last one?" he says.

That's his way of hurrying me along.

Miss Draper turns to look at him and moves her arm. The needle slips out of the vein. Damn him!

I straighten up, take a deep breath, and say, "The last one."

The struggle to get into the vein begins again. Jab, jab, jab, and then cotton balls are applied to the bleeding points.

"Bad veins, eh?" says Tom Evans.

"Yes."

Nobody pays much attention to what Miss Draper may think about people talking about her bad veins. We have more pressing business.

Tom offers to help. I decline. Finally I get the vein and

18

the treatment is given. Miss Draper is wheeled out. Dr. Evans stands dapper and polite. His graying hair is just long enough to be fashionable but not too long to annoy anyone.

"I think we'll do Mr. Marks first, Miss Moore."

"Thanks for letting me go ahead of you, Tom."

"Anytime."

He's such a nice guy. I go back to the nurses' station.

Ralph Engle is there. Ralph is a homosexual. Everybody except the patients and the referring doctors know that; the psychiatrists, the nurses, and the aides know it. He got drunk at a party at the Mapleden Country Club once and told my wife that he wished he had long blond hair that came down to his waist. His bedroom has bright purple walls. How do I know that? Because that's where the doctors leave their coats and hats when they go to the annual Christmas party he gives. Of course, he charges the party off on his income tax as a professional entertainment expense, since the guests are mainly physicians.

Ralph is a charming fellow. He really is. At a cocktail party or over a cup of coffee or anywhere but on a psychiatric ward there isn't a more agreeable chap to chat with for ten minutes. He is sitting with a few charts in front of him at the nurses' station, sipping coffee and laughing with the nurses and aides.

Ralph giggles about all his patients. If only it were a cat and dog hospital, it would be quite pleasant. But if you remember that these are patients he's discussing, it gets a little grim. It's best not to think about that.

"How's Mr. Franklin?" Ralph asks the head nurse.

"Quiet and more cooperative," Miss Spitzer replies.

"Nothing like a little basket weaving and a few tranquilizer pills to do that," Ralph replies gaily. Everyone laughs.

19

"Especially the basket weaving."

More laughter.

"Just think what pottery work is going to do for him."

A good time is had by all.

"Ralph," I say, "I notice you have Mrs. Wentworth in here. I saw her a couple of times two to three years ago. What happened to her?"

Mrs. Wentworth has had entrenched phobias for thirty-five years. I told her I thought psychiatry had little to offer her, assured her she would never be worse than she was and that people with her trouble often improve somewhat as they grow older (which is true); I sent her back to her family physician with recommendations that he give her small doses of tranquilizers from time to time and lots of reassurance.

"She decompensated," Ralph says. "Decompensation" is a word a psychiatrist uses when he hospitalizes a chronic psychoneurotic who can't afford or will not profit from office psychotherapy, but whose doctor bills will be paid by his insurance for sixty days if he is hospitalized.

"It seems she's afraid of her basement," Ralph says. "You never know what some of these people have in their basements." This amuses everyone.

"I think that's where her husband goes when he can't stand her complaining any longer. That's the trouble with these houses they build today. No basements." Ralph can go on for hours like this.

Bill Straus comes in. Irv Weiner is right behind him. Bill is a nice fellow. He's not the most brilliant man in the world, but he's honest, decent, and competent. If I ever need a psychiatrist, I think I'll go to him. He will do me no harm and I probably shall get well while I am under his care. He greets us all around, collects his charts, and goes off to a corner to read them.

Irv Weiner is Mr. Psychiatry of the Mt. Sinai group. He is

20

on every committee that has anything to do with psychiatry and thinks of himself as a noble crusader who does daily battle with the dragon Antipsychiatry. He is a tireless lecturer at women's luncheons and school meetings. He preaches resurrection by psychoanalysis and the Gospel According to St. Sigmund. He went to Harvard and married a girl from a well-known Kansas City family, as anyone discovers after talking to him for three minutes. He is smiling, patronizing, and sincere.

However, Irv is not all that goody-goody. He has a pair of Achilles' heels. He is several years older than me, and when I first went into practice, he told me how long his waiting list was and that he would send me patients. He was as good as his word, and I was grateful. But after a year I began to see the picture more clearly. He was using me as his drainoff. He had no waiting list, or a very short one, and was sending me all his lower-income patients, and the veterans of many years' treatment who would damage his reputation by not improving under his care, and other flotsam and jetsam that floated his way. Thus he satisfied his referring physicians and kept the nice, clean patients for himself.

I didn't grasp this fully until one day there arrived in my office the wife of one of the city's most prominent businessmen, referred by Irv Weiner. I sent Irv the customary ten-line thank-you note with a brief statement of her problem and my expectation that she would improve in psychotherapy. The next day I got a telephone call from him. He wanted to know exactly how she came to be referred to me and closed the conversation by saying, "I'll have to tell my new girl to check all referrals with me before sending them on." Came the dawn! I got no more referrals from Irv Weiner. He started helping some other psychiatrist get started in practice.

The ward is getting busy. Doctors are taking patients to

conference rooms for their psychotherapeutic sessions. Tom Evans has finished his eight electroshock treatments. Somebody else is doing his one or two shock treatments. Doctors are sitting in patients' rooms talking with them.

I am reading the nurses' notes and the psychologist's preliminary report on Mrs. Shapley. Miss Spitzer sits down beside me. She is an earnest, dedicated woman of about thirty.

"Dr. Chapman, what kind of activity program do you think we should organize for Mrs. Shapley?"

"I'm not sure yet."

"It seems to me," Miss Spitzer proceeds, "that she needs aggressive activities to work out her underlying hostilities. Moreover, she needs work that meets her masochistic tendencies. I think we'll put her to work scrubbing the floors and walls."

I balk and mumble evasively that she's been on the ward for only three days.

"Do you want this patient to get well, or do you want her to stagnate into even severer depression?" Miss Spitzer asks.

I've had this sort of tête-à-tête with Miss Spitzer before and I know that it's useless to present alternative views to her.

"Well," I say, "I want to talk with her another day or two, and I'll be seeing her husband again. Then we'll decide where to go with her."

"She's getting worse," Miss Spitzer continues. "At Blainton [a prominent private psychiatric hospital on the East Coast] we always moved quickly to meet the patients' needs. It's quite clear what Mrs. Shapley needs."

I knuckle under. "Very well. Do what you want, but limit it to two hours a day. Hand me one of those activity program sheets and I'll fill it out." I fill it out. Miss Spitzer walks off with her "Forgive them, Father, they know not what they do" look on her face.

Poor Miss Spitzer. I have a patient, a social worker, who knows her well. Miss Spitzer is in analysis and often leaves her analyst's office crying. She dates several black men and feels quite liberal about it, but the ones she picks (or do they pick her?) treat her like dirt. She gets very depressed for periods of several days or more. Her parents live somewhere on the East Coast and she has few friends here. She went into psychiatry to solve her own problems and I fear she is not doing too well at it. She preaches Freudian psychoanalytic psychiatry to poor unanalyzed heathen such as myself. Scrubbing floors for an hour or two a day will puzzle Mrs. Shapley and her relatives, but will do her no harm. I'll explain it as "part of the routine to take her mind off her depressed thoughts and feelings."

I go to Mrs. Shapley's room. She is sitting on the edge of the bed waiting; I close the door and sit in the chair by the window. She is thirty-four, has two children, and is married to a bossy insensitive buyer in a department store. She is depressed, thinks about suicide once in a while, has lost twelve pounds in the last sixty days, and cries a lot. When she stopped doing her housework and stared out the window, her husband ranted at her. Since that did no good, he took her to her family doctor, who sent her to me. When she told me that everyone would be better off if she were dead, I became uneasy and put her in the hospital.

This is her first depression. So I put her on imipramine, an antidepressant drug that has a 70 percent chance of clearing her depression. If she doesn't fall in the lucky 70 percent, I shall have the difficult problem of deciding whether to do psychotherapy with her or give her shock treatment. Nobody knows why imipramine clears up 70 percent of cases of this kind of depression, just as nobody understands why shock helps some people or why any of the other drugs we use work. Most such medications are discovered by hunt-and-try research teams in American and Western European pharmaceutical firms.

Lots of people understand why psychotherapy helps some patients, but unfortunately few of them can agree with one another.

Mrs. Shapley shreds a Kleenex as she fidgets in front of me. She has many problems that pills won't solve. Even when she is not depressed, she is not a happy woman, though she has a habitual smile when she is well. She was reared by cold parents, both of whom used guilt and hostility to mold her into a passive, insecure person with strong feelings of inadequacy. They did their work well. Then her husband found her. He is a strutting, domineering, heavyset man, and she mistook his authoritative manner for affectionate firmness. She meets his needs, but he does not meet hers. Finally, by the slow tabulations of those mental bookkeeping processes that we do not understand very well, it all ground on until two months ago she developed severe depressiveness. If my pills take away her melancholy thoughts and get her to doing the housework again, what can I do about the rest of her difficulties?

She probably is too passive to battle her way to a different kind of adjustment with her husband, who has merely set up with her the same kind of relationship she had with her parents. However, if in prolonged psychotherapy she can become a more self-confident, assertive person, will her marriage endure? Could her husband adjust to a wife who was more aggressive, or would the marriage deteriorate into a chronic battle that would either drive her back into a submissive role or divorce? The textbooks say that such husbands should have psychotherapy too, but long experience has taught me that these men rarely accept psychotherapy or they go only a few times and quit.

There is a good chance that we shall clear up the immediate symptoms that brought her to the hospital, but the rest of her misery is a stickier matter.

Mrs. Shapley and I talk for half an hour as we explore how she was pounded into the guilt-ridden person she is. Our talk really doesn't mean much to her now, but when her depression begins to lift, this information perhaps can be woven into more meaningful psychotherapy. Such later psychotherapy, however, depends on whether her husband lets her go on with it once she is functioning as he feels she should function at home again. "That doctor can't do anything more for you. They just keep you coming as long as they can." I explain the imminent floor scrubbing as part of the routine; she does not object.

After leaving Mrs. Shapley's room, I go down the corridor and, rapping lightly on an open door, I enter room 120. A well-groomed, good-looking woman a few years younger than myself sits on the edge of the bed, which has already been made. She smiles as I come in. I sit down on the bed a short distance away from her.

"Good morning, Judy."

"Good morning, Harry."

"Going somewhere today?" I ask as I pointedly glance at pieces of luggage by the door.

She laughs at my little joke. She is going home this morning.

"Bob will be after me at nine."

"Good old Bob," I comment. "He'll arrive on time."

She smiles, but not as broadly as before.

"Well," I go on, "this time we're going to take our little pills, just like Mrs. Chapman's little boy Harry tells us to, and we're going to live happily ever after."

"Of course," she replies, but perhaps there is something

sad in the way her smiling lips press into a thin line and the corners of her eyes narrow slightly.

"Do you know what we call those pills?" I ask with mock gravity, leaning forward slightly.

She knows that I am about to come up with one of my little witticisms, and she picks up her cue: "No, what *do* you call them?"

I put my hand to the side of my face, and behind it I whisper to her in a conspiratorial tone, "Anti-Mt.-Sinai pills. If we take them like the doctor says, we don't come back to this place—at least not for a long time, and then only when we're senile."

She laughs.

"A new ring?" I ask, noting a large blue aquamarine, set in platinum and tastefully fringed with a few small diamonds, on her left hand.

"Yes," she replies, "Bob gave it to me last night. A going-home present, I guess."

A guilt-offering, I think to myself; her husband runs around with other women when she's in the hospital.

I take the hand she stretches out to me and I squint carefully at the gem.

"From the psychiatric point of view, do you know what this means?" I ask.

"No," she says.

"It means I'm going to double the bill I send Bob."

She laughs heartily this time.

Still holding her hand, I look up at her, and as I do, my mind wanders back to a hot summer day in the middle 1930's. Judy, my brother, and I are playing Monopoly on the cool cement floor of the large front porch of the house in which I was reared. A waist-high brick wall surrounds the porch; hydrangea and spirea bushes rise alongside the wall in front of it, and honeysuckle vines on wooden trellises partially screen each end of the porch. Tall elm trees, long since killed by the Dutch elm disease, line the shady street that lies beyond the front yard, where grass is bravely trying not to wilt. It is hot, Kansas City hot; it has been over 100 every day for three weeks or more. Home air conditioning will not arrive for another decade and a half.

Judy's mother, Mrs. Rabkin, is sitting with my mother on a creaking wooden swing that is suspended by four iron chains from the beams in the roof of the porch, and she and my mother talk as they move slowly backward and forward. An electric fan whirs and jerkily rotates from one side to the other, and its cord trails across the cement floor, goes up the wall, and disappears through a small hole in the screen.

"Mrs. Chapman, you don't know how I suffer with the heat. I tell Howard every day that we should go to Minnesota or Colorado, but he says he can't get away from his business. I haven't slept at all, not a wink, for four weeks, and I'm on the verge of complete exhaustion. Judy, put your legs together and pull your skirt down. And Judy is no help. In fact, she makes my condition worse. And the colored maid left last week, and I work from morning to night, and the new girl is dirty and lazy, and it's more work to get her to do something than to do it myself. Judy, don't laugh so loud, and don't pick your nose like that. You have no idea, Mrs. Chapman, how noise frays my nerves. And Judy is so noisy, and Howard turns the radio so loud to listen to those baseball games. I say to him, 'What's more important, my health or those baseball games?' But he doesn't pay any attention, and, like I said, Judy is no help at all. I got on the streetcar the other day, coming back from downtown, and Judy had to stand, it was so crowded. With my physical condition I couldn't stand, so I took the only seat there was, and at Thirty-ninth and Main, when the car stopped all of a sudden, Judy stepped on my foot. It bruised

27

me horribly. Look, you can still see the bruise. I didn't sleep for two days because of the pain. Mrs. Yudkin was on the car next to me, she's Ruth Lerner's mother, and she said, 'When they're young they step on your feet, and when they're older they step on your heart.' And that's the way it is. Judy has no consideration for my condition, and when she's older she'll forget me altogether. Dr. Cordell says that if my varicose veins go on like this, I could get a leg ulcer, and you know that they never heal. Mrs. Leidig has had one for years; it has a horrid smell. Judy, get me a glass of cold water. No, Harry, let Judy do it. She never does anything to help me, no matter how sick I am or how bad I feel. The pitcher is over there. No, the other one is my glass. I've seen Dr. Campbell twice this month. If the shots don't help me, he says he may have to operate again. I hope it's not cancer. It runs in my family. Judy, you're spilling the water. Don't run. Can't you ever be careful? And your dress is all wrinkled and smudged, and I ironed it this morning. I got up early to do it, before it got hot. Mrs. Chapman, like I said, she never has any consideration for me. She only thinks of herself."

Unlike the vast majority of psychiatrists, I practice in the same city and district of it in which I was reared. After a psychiatrist spends twelve to fifteen years in college, medical school, internship, residency training, and, as in the case of myself and many others, military service, it's rare that he returns to practice in the same city in which he was reared; it is rarer still that he practices in the same district of that city. I have known some of my patients since childhood. Judy is one of them.

She was the only child of a complaining, self-centered mother who whined her way through life, until she died in her middle seventies. Judy's father was a businessman who spent little time at home. In the 1930's he owned three optical stores in downtown Kansas City, and between 1940 and 1960 he became wealthy by installing optical departments in leased spaces in a nationwide chain of department stores. He was out of town almost constantly from the late 1930's onward. It was general knowledge that he had mistresses in two or three cities and casual girlfriends in many more.

Thus, Judy was reared without love from either of her parents, and she was pounded continually by the reproaches and harangues of her mother. As a child, she was awkward, apprehensive, and anxious to please, and she had a constant smile that said, "Don't hurt me." I didn't see much of her for a number of years, but when I came home from medical school on vacations during the middle 1940's, I found she had grown into a pretty, shy, graceful girl. I dated her a few times. Then she turned me down, saying that her parents liked me and said that I sould be a fine professional man, but they didn't want her to risk becoming serious about a non-Jewish boy. In time, she married Bob Ehrlich. He now runs her father's business, travels a lot, and has, as I know from well-documented gossip, her father's ways with women. I suspect that Judy knows, too.

After the birth of her first child, Judy became very agitated. She talked constantly, and even after she became hoarse from continual chatter, she continued her croaking monologue. She flitted in aimless physical movement from one uncompleted task to another, and her thoughts poured out in a senseless jumble. She ate little and slept two to three hours a night. She laughed, sang, and joked in a forced, artificial way, but occasionally she lapsed into sobbing despair for a minute or two. She said that her pediatrician was Jesus Christ, but she soon abandoned that idea for the more persistent delusion that her child was the long-awaited Messiah.

Depending on which school of psychiatry you belong to and which particular psychiatric authorities you deify, we

29

have a choice of labels to stick on this type of illness and various ways to explain it. However, regardless of what you call it and how you interpret it, we have effective pharmacological treatment for it. After three weeks of hospital care the patient usually is much improved, and after six to eight weeks he in almost all cases recovers and goes home. Judy has had three such illnesses, and I have taken care of her during the last two of them; when she had her first one, I was in military service, during the Korean War. Such disorders tend to be repetitive, occurring at intervals of from a few years to two or three decades.

Why do people get these illnesses? We have a smorgasbord of psychiatric theories in answer to that. We can cite the speculations of Freudian psychoanalysis, or neo-Freudian psychoanalysis, or interpersonal theory, or behavior theory, or organic theory, or Jungian theory, or existential theory, or communication theory, or many others. Judy has had several years of psychotherapy with elegant, expensive gentlemen who present intricate papers at psychiatric conventions, but when she gets extremely sick they bring her to me, and I do what works.

In the final analysis, it's the patients who keep our profession more or less chained to reality.

And so I come back to Mrs. Rabkin endlessly complaining about her health, her daughter, and her hardships to my mother on a front-porch swing on a hot summer day, and to Mr. Rabkin in his undershirt chewing cigars while he listens to baseball games on the radio, paying little attention to both his wife and his daughter. And I look at the handsome, middle-aged woman beside me, who was reared without love or understanding or kindness.

"The nurses will give you a two-week supply of medication as you leave," I say. "Call Marie for an appointment. If you don't call her, I'll tell her to call you. And let's make this the last one of these things. I'm getting too old to make hospital rounds at this time of the morning."

She laughs, and I leave.

I go back to the nurses' station, where Ralph Engle has everybody in stitches with a hilarious account of how a painter fell off a ladder while working on his summer cottage at Lake Mitaconga on the outskirts of Kansas City.

I listen to that for a minute or two. Miss Moore is handing coffee around; I decline a cup and reflect that Mr. Temple is a fool if he doesn't marry her. I wonder if they are already sleeping together. My revery, which trails off into the details of this, is broken by Alex Weil, who sticks his head in the door and says, "Miss Moore, I think we can do Mrs. Morgan's treatment now."

I write brief progress notes on the charts of my four patients. Mr. Rattner is beginning to improve with shock treatment, as expected. Miss Draper is only slightly improved, and transfer to a public hospital for long-term care will be recommended to her family. Mrs. Shapley has been started on imipramine with a good chance of recovery from her depression, and supportive psychotherapy is being carried out. Mrs. Ehrlich is discharged as "recovered" and I sign the discharge sheet.

I fill in a few incomplete parts of the admission workup on Mrs. Shapley, check the results of her routine laboratory tests, and slide the charts across the desk. The ward secretary, a black college student, picks them up and puts them in their proper slots in the rotating file holder.

"Buzz me out, please, Miss Nelson," and I walk toward the door that leads from the psychiatric ward into the main part of the hospital. As I reach the door, there is a loud whizzing noise that tells me that Miss Nelson has pushed the button that unlocks the door. I push it open and leave, and it clicks shut behind me.

31

2

8:00. I walk down to the coffee shop to spend five minutes over a cup of coffee. I must keep my political fences mended. Hospital coffee shops are where specialists keep in touch with their referring physicians and stay abreast of professional gossip. I go in and sit down at a table with Jack Kramer, Norman Gold, and Tony Adams: two internists and an ear-nose-and-throat man.

They grunt greetings at me and go on with their discussion of a vital topic. The board of trustees of Mt. Sinai want to hire two full-time radiologists on a salary basis to take over the X-ray department. This would leave the current radiologists, Drs. Levy and Stern, with their office practice only (they are partners), and all the hospital work would be in the hands of the hospital's salaried radiologists.

One of the nightmares that haunt American doctors is that hospitals may gradually replace the private attending physicians with salaried physicians on contract and that the fees for their services will be paid directly to the hospital. Boards of directors often see this as a good way to end their annual deficits and to offer comprehensive, systematic services to their patients at lower costs. The doctors see this scheme as socialized medicine in which the patients will get slipshod care from bureaucratic hacks who will have no real interest in or personal knowledge of the patients.

"If they get away with this in radiology, they'll want to do the same thing in surgery, internal medicine, and every other department," Jack Kramer says.

"It's just plain socialized medicine," Tony Adams adds.

"How any American who believes in the free-enterprise system can even think of such a thing is beyond me," Jack continues. "Those bastards on the board of directors are all fat-cat businessmen and lawyers, and if we suggested to one of them that all the lawyers in town be put on government salaries and assigned cases as they came in the door, or that all their factories and stores be turned over to the government, they'd think we'd gone stark raving nuts. But when it comes to medicine, oh, that's a different matter, they say. The hell it's different! We're defending the system that has made this country what it is."

"No doubt about that," I say with a cheery smile. Jack looks at me as if he thought there was something sinister hidden in my remark.

"Balls!" says Jack Kramer. The precise meaning of this remark remains somewhat obscure, but it accurately conveys Jack's mood of irritability and disgust.

"I cornered Jerry Lowenstein the other night at a party," he continues, "and I told him that he and the other directors are playing with dynamite on this issue. What the hell would they do if the doctors all resigned? And that's how it is. Why, Mort Levy was one of the first doctors on this staff when they opened the doors, and he's devoted his whole life to giving this hospital a damned good X-ray department. Now they want to throw him out and put in some young jerk who'll work for nothing and do lousy X rays in his place. You spend your whole life serving the public, and then what do you get? They kick you in the teeth. Old Nick Haldane was right. He always gave them a bill right after he put a cast on or sewed them up. 'Hit them while the tears are in their eyes,' he used to say. 'Today you're a hero and the next day you're a bum.'" The late Nicholas Haldane was a highly successful Kansas City orthopedist who died eight years ago shortly after he finished building a home that cost $250,000.

I feel it's best to stir my coffee and not comment on the lines of reasoning that Jack Kramer is pursuing in several directions.

However, since I do not join in vehemently, Norman Gold turns to me and says, "Some hospitals in the East are employing full-time psychiatrists. That would end hospital practice for you."

"If the whole medical staff sticks together and the medical society backs us up, they can't do it," I put in. That pleases them. Now I'm one of the boys. Psychiatrists are always a little suspect on this crucial issue, since a significant percentage of them already work as salaried employees in state psychiatric hospitals, child-guidance clinics, and various other kinds of public and private institutions.

There is very little chance that the Mt. Sinai board of directors will make this change. The doctors are united against it, and several of them are related by blood or marriage to the businessmen, attorneys, and socially prominent women who form the hospital's directorate. The issue will die in one of the various committees that must pass on the matter.

I point this out and tell Norman Gold that he should go to work on his wife's brother, who is on the board. This pleases Norman. It emphasizes to us all how well connected he is.

"I intend to talk to him about it." he says. However, he may not. His wife dominates him and he'll do it only if she lets him. I know a good deal about what goes on in the Gold domicile. I treated their adolescent son a few years back.

Ed Pearl comes over, making the rounds of the tables. Ed does about one-third of the general surgery at Mt. Sinai, splitting the fees squarely with his referring physicians. He's a smooth politician and he married into a large, well-known family. He has a back-slapping acquaintance-ship with three hundred doctors and he remembers at least one or two central facts about each of them. He puts his hand on my shoulder and leans across toward each of us for a moment. "How's that girl of yours doing in med school?" "Congratulations on making the golf finals at the club." "I told you General Dynamics would go up when you bought one hundred shares of it." Having exchanged comments with all of us, he moves on to the next table. However, if I ever had to have my belly opened at Mt. Sinai, I'd have Ed do it. He's a good surgeon.

I get up, pay my check, and leave. It's 8:10. I get on the elevator and go to the fourth floor, where I have a consultation to do, an orthopedic consultation case.

These cases turn my stomach and I refuse them when I can, but Dan Baum called me yesterday and requested this one. I can't turn Dan down. He set my daughter's arm when she broke it and fixed my son's feet when they turned inward during infancy.

I go to the nurses' station. By chance, Dan Baum is there; he introduces me to Mr. Herbert Kassman, the patient's attorney, who explains that he dropped by the hospital on his way downtown to his office to have the patient sign some papers. Mr. Kassman greets me with unctuous blatancy and takes over the conversation.

He is very anxious to impress on me how much this patient is suffering because of his back injury, and without inquiry on my part, he assures me that my fee will be paid promptly upon receipt of my report. Dan tries to break in to give some medical data, but Mr. Kassman pushes him aside. He explains what a good thing it is that he bumped

35

into Dan and me on the ward. This is a tough case. The opposition are Montgomery, Lambkin and Phillips, attorneys for the insurance company. A very experienced firm, he states. Undoubtedly I've heard of them? I have.

Mr. Kassman confides that Montgomery, Lambkin and Phillips have compiled a lot of data that may hurt our case. They have established that the patient has a problem with alcohol, but they cannot prove that he was intoxicated when he fell off that first-floor scaffolding of the building he was working on. In fact, it is certain that he could not have been drunk, or the foreman would not have let him onto the job that morning two years ago.

"Two years ago?" I ask.

Yes, it's dragged on. The patient has been receiving compensation and the matter is due to come up in court for a final decision within a few months, unless it's settled out of court. A psychiatric opinion is needed to counter the opposition's claim that his alcoholic problem had something to do with his fall from the scaffolding. They can show that he has been a member of Alcoholics Anonymous twice and has had one arrest for driving while intoxicated. There's no question about his having had a problem with alcohol, but it has no connection with his injury and incapacitation.

"Incapacitation?" I begin.

"Yes, incapacitation." Mr. Kassman speeds on, stabbing his right forefinger into the palm of his left hand to emphasize whatever points he feels are most telling. "And no one, no one," he repeats, "can tell how long the incapacitation will continue. We're suing for two hundred and fifty thousand dollars. The man has a wife and three children, one married."

I know the system, and I've been the accomplice of more compensation lawyers than I like to remember; as a breed, I do not recommend them. They work on the basis of a fifty-fifty split with the patient. Whatever the settlement, from a pittance to a fortune, the lawyer gets a clear 50 percent. The longer the case drags on, the higher the final settlement tends to be. When the final settlement is greatly delayed, any psychological overlay in the patient's symptoms tends to grow bigger and more firmly fixed. The benefit of this to the lawyer is obvious, since psychologically caused disability is just as compensable as physically caused disability; the tragedy of it to the patient is less apparent. Moreover, even if the patient has a poor case or no case at all, the lawyer knows that after a couple of years the insurance company will settle it out of court for a few thousand dollars simply to get rid of the dragging expenses and nuisance of the matter. In this particular case the final settlement will probably be a fifth, or much less, of the sum they're suing for, and the odds are that it will be settled out of court two or three days before the final hearing is due. This horrid system will never be changed so long as state legislatures are composed mainly of lawyers.

Dan Baum fills me in from the orthopedic point of view. The man had a crushed vertebra and nothing else orthopedically; it healed completely a year and a half ago and this injury cannot explain the patient's pain, his limp, and his inability to work. There must be something else.

"Now, Doctor," Mr. Kassman goes on, "we just want a report to the effect that any tendency to occasional alcoholic excess has no bearing on this man's orthopedic injuries. No other issue need be dealt with. Also, let's delay treatment until after the patient's financial interests are taken care of." In other words, if he improves medically, Mr. Kassman's case will be weakened and both he and the patient will receive less money. The hideous rub of the matter is that after these cases drag on two to three years the patient often remains incapacitated for many months or years after the financial settlement. I've seen men and

37

women who were still disabled by the psychological overlays of long-healed physical injuries ten years after their litigation was terminated and the final sum had been paid.

Dan looks at me a little apologetically and says, "You call it as you see it, Harry."

"That's right," Mr. Kassman says. "We want an unbiased medical report to help this poor man and his family. Come on. I'll introduce you to him, so you can get his full cooperation in the examination."

He is quite right on that point. Most compensation patients view psychiatrists as enemies who are out to prove that they are either faking or are mentally deranged. Hence they rarely cooperate well in psychiatric examinations, and many of them refuse to cooperate at all.

Mr. Kassman presents me to a thin, unshaven working-man sitting on the edge of his bed in a six-bed ward.

"This is Dr. Chapman. He's on our side. Answer anything he asks you." He leaves.

I sit down and get the same story I've heard a few dozen times before from a few dozen other patients. I take careful notes. I'll need them for my report and, if it comes to that, for my courtroom testimony. I get the details of his accident and the list of company doctors who, he says, mishandled his case and gave him the wrong treatments. Then he gives me the names of the private physicians of his own choice whom he has seen, ending with Dr. Baum, whom he first saw four weeks ago. Mr. Kassman entered the picture six months after the accident; when the company tried to settle the matter for five thousand dollars, his father-in-law told him he'd be a fool to sign anything until he saw a lawyer, and he recommended Mr. Kassman.

Then I ask about his problem with alcohol and get the usual mess of contradictory statements and evasions. Yes, he has been to Alcoholics Anonymous, but that was long ago. He was on the wagon at the time of the injury. Yes, the company's lawyers have dug up a report at the municipal hospital saying that he was there with delirium tremens four years ago, but that was not so. He was just nervous over some trouble with his wife. Has she ever left him? Well, yes, but they are back together again.

During the examination I have made notes on the usual things lawyers want to know about. His memory is good, his emotional reactions, despite his defensiveness, are appropriate, his thought processes are unimpaired, and he is well oriented as to time, place, and person. All this has little bearing on the central problems he has and the treacherous future that lies before him, but the law, blinkered and plodding with its eyes on the narrow lane before it, has its own ideas about what is and is not relevant. More than once I have been told by squinting judges, "Kindly answer only what is asked, Doctor," and "Such things are not relevant to the issue."

I check a few points in the neurological examination, and I say that Dr. Baum undoubtedly will have a neurologist examine him. Yes, Dr. Schaller has already seen him and has tapped his reflexes and all that, he says.

After filling a page and a half with notes, I tell him that is all and that I'll send a report to his lawyer. He tells me that he signed a permission form that morning authorizing me to send information to Mr. Kassman and to no one else. I say that his lawyer undoubtedly will send that form to me. I rise to go.

"What do you think, Doc?" he asks.

"About your condition?"

"Yeah."

"Well, I think you had a back injury. I do not think your problem with alcohol has anything to do with it. However, I think there's a big emotional overlay in your symptoms now. In other words, I think that the worry and tension you have about your injury, and your legal problems, and all this trouble over money, are more important in your symptoms right now than any bone injury. It's mainly muscle tension; you have muscle tension because you're tense."

I know the futility of telling these things to him, but it is my duty to answer his questions. He becomes angry and suspicious.

"You mean you think I'm faking?"

"No, I didn't say that. I just mean that muscle tension is causing eighty percent or more of your back pain, and your back muscles are tense because you're tense."

"But it's all because of my accident, isn't it?" he says, staring hard at me. "I never had backaches before that accident, and I walked straight and I could work. But I can't now."

"Your accident precipitated all this," I say.

"You mean, it *caused* all this," he says, setting me straight.

"Yes, but if you'd stop worrying about yourself and unwind, you'd get better sooner."

There are five men in the other beds who have been watching the proceedings, and one says, "I told you that you shouldn't talk to any psychiatrist, Fred."

Fred looks at him apprehensively. "My lawyer said he's all right."

"Look, Fred," I say, "there will be nothing in my report that will hurt you. The insurance company's lawyers are trying to blame it all on your history of drinking. The drinking has nothing to do with this problem. I'll say that. That's the main point Mr. Kassman wants settled. He has to have a psychiatrist's opinion saying that to throw at the insurance company and their lawyers."

Fred looked a little less belligerent.

I shook hands with him and walked out.

40

I went back to the nurses' station and wrote a brief note in Fred's chart: "Examined patient at request of Dr. Daniel Baum. A report in detail will be sent to Dr. Baum and to the patient's attorney." A psychiatrist does not put more than that in the chart of a patient who is engaged in litigation, since a chart can be subpoenaed.

As I left the nurses' station, Dan Baum came back.

"What do you think?"

I told him.

"Sorry to call you on a case like this, but Kassman sends me a lot of patients, and occasionally we need a psychiatrist's report."

"Give this man a little muscle-relaxing physiotherapy and a lot of reassurance," I said.

"Okay."

However, we both knew that it would do no good until the financial issues were solved, and that might be several months or more away. Also, by that time Fred might have gone through the hands of one or two more doctors. Compensation patients often are distrustful of their physicians and change them frequently.

I walked to the elevator and went down to the main floor. As I got off the elevator, I saw my number flashing on the overhead black box of the doctors' call system. Sixty-seven. Sixty-seven. It flashed once every five seconds, and several other numbers blinked at other times.

I went to the doctors' lounge and picked up one of the phones on a long table against the wall.

"This is Dr. Chapman. Any messages?"

"Two of them. Call Mrs. Crawford at 444-5719 and Dr. Mason at St. Catharine's."

I called Dr. Mason first, and after a minute or so the operator at St. Catharine's found him. Dr. Mason is an internist with a large practice. I identified myself.

"Harry, this is George Mason. I have a patient in room

three fifteen here at St. Catharine's whom I'd like you to see. She has a lot of symptoms that I think have a large functional component. Maybe you can do something for her."

I asked for her name.

"Helen McLaughlin. She's about fifty."

I felt queasy and scratched her room number off the pad in front of me.

"Look, George, I've seen her before. I saw her a couple of years ago; she's a very difficult woman."

"I didn't know that," he said. "Well, then, I don't need to give you much more data on her. She needs a little more help."

Mrs. McLaughlin was an immature, demanding woman who for thirty years had had anxiety attacks and phobias; there was a strong hysterical overlay in her symptoms. She had had four years of thrice-weekly psychotherapy with Marvin Crosswell on the South Side of Kansas City; it ended when she could no longer afford him. This treatment did her no good. In fact, it quite possibly harmed her. The sullen pouts she had when she was crossed by her husband or her adolescent children gradually deteriorated into screaming rages, since they acquired the status of "symptoms" rather than "temper fits." Under Dr. Crosswell she became a periodic wrist scratcher with razor blades, and occasionally she took half a dozen sedative tablets in a suicidal gesture. She dominated her husband and flailed her children by these techniques. Before psychotherapy she had been a difficult but tolerable woman; after it she was a tyrant who used psychiatry to intimidate everyone around her.

"George," I said, "I can't do anything for this woman. Psychiatry has nothing to offer her. In fact, I feel that this type of patient sometimes gets worse in psychiatric treatment."

42

"Well, what the hell am I to do with her?" he asked. "She's fine as long as she stays here on the medical service of St. Catharine's, but when I send her home she goes to pot, and she or her husband calls me twice a day."

"She's been like that for years," I replied lamely.

"Harry, you're the one to take care of her. I know you can't cure her, but you can keep her afloat. Give her some kind of supportive care. I have a lot of cardiac cases I can't cure, but I give them supportive care. Somebody has to take care of this woman. They can afford it. They'll pay your bills."

"George, I've got enough of these cases already. Send her to one of the boys on the South Side."

"Oh, hell," he replied, "those bastards will psychoanalyze her until the house is mortgaged and the kids have to drop out of college. She thinks it's great, but I'd send her to the chiropractors first."

"George, there's a new young fellow in town. Jackson. Terry Jackson. He's decent. He'll struggle with her for a while and not hurt them too much in the process. He needs the patients. He'll take her off your hands."

"Okay. What's his number?"

"I don't know. He's not in the phone book yet. But the medical society has his number and office address. He's somewhere on the Plaza. Terrence Jackson."

"All right. Thanks, Harry."

"Look, George, I'll do a little more than that. I'll call Jackson and I'll tell him exactly what the picture is. I'll also tell him to set a three-month time limit with both her and her husband as a trial period of therapy, and if everything is still a mess at the end of three months to urge the husband to send her to a state hospital on a ninety-day commitment. He ought to be able to arrange it on a woman who has scratched her wrists with razor blades as many times as she has. They'll have half a dozen emergency-room records to present as evidence. I've seen some of these cases quiet down to a certain extent after three to four months in a state hospital. When these hysterical personalities know that there's a stone wall somewhere, they may slow down and get along better. I don't have the time to go through all this, with the court hearing and the rest of it, but Jackson does. He's a good kid. He'll listen to what I tell him, and if he has any doubts about it, he'll lose them when he's struggled with her for three months."

"Okay. I'll call him. Thanks."

"Good-bye, George."

I hung up. I was doing the same thing to Terry Jackson that Irv Weiner had done to me during my first year in practice. I was using him as a drainoff for my undesirable referrals.

I sat for a minute or so and doodled on the pad of note paper before me. I was not feeling too comfortable with myself.

Anyway, the McLaughlins would pay their bills, they would help keep the wolf away from Terry Jackson's door, and somebody had to grapple with Mrs. McLaughlin during whatever kind of crisis she was going through. In addition, I told myself that I was being more honest with Jackson than Weiner had been with me. Moreover, there's a limit to what a psychiatrist who doesn't hide behind all that flimsy theory can take from his patients. A woman like Mrs. McLaughlin puts a psychiatrist through the wringer if he looks at her as something more than "an interesting case of unresolved oedipal transference" or, worse still, a wobbly ego with a bank balance.

I wrote in my pocket notebook: "Call Jackson—Helen McLaughlin—three-month trial of treatment and then state hospital."

Then I called Mrs. Crawford. She thought she was pregnant. Could she go on taking her phenothiazine

44

medication? Yes, I said, she could. Would it damage the baby? No, I assured her, it would not. She said that she had read an article in the newspaper that said. . . . I reassured her that it didn't make any difference what the article in the paper said. Some drugs were dangerous, but this one was not. There was nothing to worry about. Yes, I was 100 percent sure.

Mrs. Crawford is an attractive woman of twenty-four. She had a manic psychosis and got over it in six weeks on an antipsychotic medication and supportive psychotherapy. However, it was advisable to continue to take the medication for several months more, since it much decreased the chance of a relapse. She thanked me.

I felt better. When I was in my first year of psychiatric residency, we had a third-year resident who probably taught me more than any of the senior staff. He once said, "There are two kinds of patients—the ones you help and the ones you learn something from."

Mrs. Crawford and Mrs. McLaughlin.

I took my psychiatric residency training in a large university medical center. The psychiatric department occupied most of an eight-story building, which was part of a maze of interlocking hospitals and laboratory buildings that covered most of three city blocks. I spent three and a half years there and would have stayed on longer as a junior staff member had not the Korean War hustled me into military service.

Our chief of staff was a hulking, physically awkward man with bright red hair that he cut short, like stubble. He had been reared a devout Catholic in a small town in upstate New York, and in late adolescence he had gone away on a scholarship to Cornell, where he got his education and lost his religion. Having so painfully gained and lost one set of beliefs, he was careful never to believe in anything again. Nevertheless, he had an aching void in the place where his faith had been; trying to fill it, he wandered into psychiatry, but he found no answers there. He tested all psychiatric theories against the yardstick of logic and in the end concluded that all of them were as ridiculous as the Catholicism in which he had been reared.

In teaching, he liked to point out wryly that if you thought about it carefully, there was not much difference between id, ego, and superego and Father, Son, and Holy Ghost, and that the concept of the Oedipus complex, if stripped of its pseudoscientific trimmings, bore a remarkable resemblance to the doctrine of original sin. He marveled that it was strange that nature, at least in psychiatry, always contrived to construct everything in trinities.

He pointed out, as Sir Carl Popper later demonstrated more systematically, that all psychiatric theories, from psychoanalysis to existential theory, were so set up that they could be neither proved nor disproved. All their basic propositions were like the statement, "All events are controlled by Divine Providence." Much human experience could be cited both to support and attack this statement, but it was so set up that it could never be proved or disproved and hence forever would remain a matter of faith rather than a science. In addition to considering all schools of psychiatry rubbish, he quoted the many statistical studies that showed that if a series of patients was unselected and large enough, the percentage of patients who improved or got well in psychotherapy was not much different from the percentage of patients who spontaneously improved or got well without any treatment at all.

He was both the best and the worst teacher I had. He taught me a gentle tolerance for all psychiatric viewpoints and the danger of becoming dogmatically committed to any one of them, but in dealing with patients he was probably the worst psychiatrist I ever knew. People traveled hundreds of miles to consult him when they could have got sounder opinions from their family physicians. Our chief was erudite, he was an excellent writer, and he had a national reputation, but with a patient in front of him he was a bumbling, embarrassed, inarticulate man whose clinical judgment was awful. He hid behind a pipe that he constantly was engaged in either filling or emptying and that steadfastly refused to stay lit. This gave him something to do during consultations, and it concealed his confusion from the patients and their relatives. Because of his position he had to do a fair amount of consultation work, but I doubt that he had treated a patient in twenty years. He made recommendations and referred the patients for treatment by one of his subordinates, who almost invariably ignored both his opinions and suggestions.

In addition to our chief, we had two other full professors. One was Dr. Wilenz. He was an enthusiastic proponent of "learning theory," the grandfather of that strapping adolescent "behavior theory," which today is attracting so much attention. Except for the first twenty minutes of an interview with a patient, Dr. Wilenz talked continually. His admirers called him eloquent, and his exasperated opponents called him garrulous. No matter what a patient's problems were, Dr. Wilenz could jam them into the neat, square pigeonholes of learning theory. After examining a patient for twenty minutes with well-loaded questions, he lit into him. He explained his problems to him in an impressive lecture that left the patient perplexed or depressed or furious. Dr. Wilenz couldn't talk to children and adolescents at all, and he blushed when a patient mentioned sex. He was a nationally recognized authority on psychosomatic medicine, but he had a duodenal ulcer that most embarrassingly hemorrhaged from time to time, causing him to be admitted to the same medical floors on which he taught. This, however, in no way diminished his confidence in either himself or learning theory. His messianic fervor infuriated the psychoanalysts. At one memorable staff meeting one of our senior psychoanalytic consultants grew so angry and agitated that he literally trembled and stammered in rage as he rose to refute everything that Dr. Wilenz had said.

The third of our full professors was a psychoanalyst, Dr. Gower; he ran the child-guidance clinic. He viewed everyone who did not believe every last word that Freud wrote (except that awkward business about the death instinct) as a benighted heathen to be baptized and converted. During the first three to four months in which the young resident psychiatrist worked under him, Dr. Gower was gracious, patronizing, and informative. He laid the intricate doctrines of psychoanalysis before the novitiate with charm and skill. Then, if the novitiate did not accept it all or, God forbid, asked difficult questions, Dr. Gower's gentleness turned to irritability and occasionally to downright anger. When psychiatrists get mad they do not call one another names; instead they hurl diagnoses at one another. Hence, the recalcitrant novitiate was told that his orally fixated personality problems prevented him from seeing patients' difficulties clearly, or that his anally caused compulsiveness crippled him as a therapist, or that his Oedipus complex was in such hopeless disarray that the young doctor should consider going into some other specialty where he would do less damage, such as anesthesiology or dermatology. If, on the other hand, the young psychiatrist knuckled under, either in sincere conversion or diplomatic compromise, and mouthed the proper Freudian phrases, the sun of Dr. Gower's pleasure shone. I shammed with him for one year and learned a great deal, for he knew a lot about children and adolescents and was a good teacher.

Beneath these three full professors were a number of

48

other full-time psychiatrists. On the whole, the most capable of them were the younger ones who had finished their residencies and were spending a few years as instructors or assistant professors before they went into the more lucrative field of private practice. They taught me more about day-to-day work with patients than the top men; though their erudition was less, their clinical judgment tended to be better. One by one they left, usually going to distant cities, and for a brief time after the end of my residency training I was one of them.

Of course, we had our devil. I shall call him Dr. Martin; a timely coronary has long since carried him to his reward. During the last years of the Great Depression of the 1930's, when it was difficult to go into private practice, he served as a psychiatrist in the Army, and during the Second World War he became a colonel. After being discharged in late 1945, he decided to go into private practice, and he figured that the best way to do it was first to become established in the city of his choice as a member of the medical-school faculty there. Using his background as one of the top administrators of psychiatric services in the Army during the Second World War, and aided by recommendations from some of the prominent psychiatrists who had served under him or alongside him, he had no trouble getting our chief to take him on as an associate professor. He spent two years on the full-time teaching staff while establishing contacts with many internists and other referring physicians. He then resigned his full-time position and went into private practice while maintaining his university affiliation by teaching residents three or four hours a week. He was in this latter stage when he was my teacher for four months.

Dr. Martin was a mercenary fraud. Although he did not believe in psychotherapy, he knew it was fashionable, and so he advocated it and taught it. For every psychotherapeutic problem he had a cliché, and in time we residents labeled them "Martinisms." A few choice items from his large store of meaningless dicta were: "Play it by ear," "Give this patient some rope," "Tighten the reins on her a little," "Let's let this run its course," "Now is the time to zero in on the problem," "Gently does it," "Let this cool off for a while," "Separate the wheat from the chaff," and "Yank it out by the roots." If a young resident pressed hard to discover how he should translate these adages into things he actually said to a patient during an interview, Dr. Martin leaned back in his chair with a knowing smile and said, "That's what you must work out for yourself, face-to-face with the patient. No two patients are exactly alike." The residents, depending on their personalities, regarded him with camouflaged disgust or open hostility. When he went into private practice, he had a six-figure income the first year.

Many other men and women, in small and large ways, contributed to my psychiatric education. One of the most influential was a young psychiatrist from Baltimore who had studied directly under Harry Stack Sullivan and worked alongside me in military service. He had an uncanny ability in understanding schizophrenics. He later published a few papers in the psychiatric journals, and committed suicide in his early forties.

During the first week of my psychiatric training we had two group orienting sessions with our chief. On each occasion he ambled through an hour of contradictory statements while fiddling with his pipe, and he fielded our questions in clumsy ways. At the end of the second session he handed each of us a two-page mimeographed reading list, but implied that we were not to take it too seriously.

"It's the patients who will teach you psychiatry," he ended. "Spend as much time with them as you can."

He was right.

Mrs. Crawford and Mrs. McLaughlin.

3

ABOUT 9:15 I got into my car and drove to St. Catharine's. The morning snow had been light and traffic moved easily. I organize my day to avoid rush-hour congestion, and the places I go are no more than ten minutes' driving distance from each other. I went in and flicked on my call light to tell the switchboard operator that I was in the hospital, in case there were any calls for me.

The atmosphere at St. Catharine's is different from that at Mt. Sinai. The frugal, meticulous nuns keep their hospital calm and very neat. There is none of the hurly-burly of Mt. Sinai. Even though there are far fewer sisters than ten years ago, they still set the tone of St. Catharine's.

Statuettes of saints gaze from wall niches at the elevator stops, and oil paintings of long-dead Kansas City bishops line the walls of the main lobby. A crucifix is on the wall in every room. The chapel and convent quarters adjoin the hospital building, and about ten nuns occupy key administrative and nursing positions.

As soon as I turned on my call light, my number began to flash. Ninety-three. Ninety-three. I went back to the doctors' lounge and picked up the phone.

"Dr. Chapman here. Any messages?"

"Sister Margaret Dabney would like to see you, Doctor." At St. Catharine's everybody has his title and it is frequently used. A doctor is called doctor, a sister is called sister, and nurses and aides are more commonly addressed as Mrs. and Mr. then at Mt. Sinai. One sees more Ms.'s on nurses' and aides' nameplates at Mt. Sinai than at St. Catharine's.

"Sister Margaret Dabney," I repeated dully. Then I remembered who she was and tightened up. "Do you know where she is right now?" I asked.

"She's probably in the admission office, Doctor. I'll check and either she or I will call you right back." I hung up. In less than a minute the phone rang.

"This is Sister Margaret Dabney."

"Yes, Sister."

"I am Mrs. Kennedy's sister. Do you remember?"

"Yes, Sister, I remember. I am very sorry about what happened."

"Thank you, Doctor." She stumbled a little. "I know you are very busy, Doctor, but could I see you for a minute? I would appreciate it very much. I just want to ask a question or two."

"Certainly, Sister, anytime. Now or whenever is best for you. I'll be here for at least another hour and a half, perhaps until noon."

"Now would be fine, Doctor. Could we meet outside the director's office? There's a conference room next to it. I'll get the key."

"I'll be waiting for you, Sister."

"Thank you, Doctor." The nuns of St. Catharine's are very formal, especially to authoritative figures. Doctors are authorities. St. Luke was a doctor.

I went across the hall and waited outside the director's office. I knew fairly well what Sister Margaret Dabney had in mind.

Four years ago her sister, Mrs. Kennedy, had been my

52

patient. She was a woman in her early twenties who had developed a schizophrenic illness during the first few days after giving birth to her first child. Her husband, a red-faced, stocky laborer, had brought her to the hospital from the small town in Iowa in which they lived. He had asked his wife's sister, Sister Margaret Dabney, to recommend a psychiatrist. She had recommended me, and Mrs. Kennedy had been hospitalized on the psychiatric ward of St. Catharine's. With an antipsychotic medication and some supportive counseling she had recovered in about six weeks. She had continued to see me in follow-up visits for a year more on an outpatient basis.

Twelve months afterward she again appeared at the hospital. Four weeks previously she had had her second child, and two weeks after delivery she had lapsed into a second schizophrenic psychosis. She talked incoherently about the Blessed Mother and the Sacred Heart, and she alternated between sobbing depressiveness and excited agitation. I again treated her with an antipsychotic medication and supportive interview work, and she once more recovered. However, when she went home, she began to deteriorate, and within a month she was back in the hospital in a full-blown relapse. This happened twice more before she had a persistent recovery.

When she was firmly well, I had a conference with her and her husband. I told them that, as was obvious, she had had identical psychoses following the births of two children. I told them that we sometimes see cases like this and that although we don't know why, some women have a special vulnerability to psychiatric illnesses in the postpartum period. Such illnesses perhaps were caused by some psychological factors about which we could only speculate or some physiologic difficulties that we did not understand, but one thing was clinically certain: A woman who had such illnesses after two deliveries had an uncomfortably high risk of having a third one after a third delivery.

Then I came to the nitty-gritty of the matter. I told them that I was aware that each of them came from a devout Catholic family; I knew that he had a brother who was a priest and that she had two sisters who were nuns, one of whom was Sister Margaret Dabney at St. Catharine's. But as a physician it was my duty to point out to them the severe danger of their having any more children. I emphasized that her recovery from her second illness had been much slower and more difficult than from her first one. I indicated that during her second illness I had for a time considered it quite possible that she would end up a long-term patient in a state psychiatric hospital. However, happily she had recovered.

I said that though I was Protestant, I clearly understood the reasoning behind the Catholic point of view and perhaps at times could sympathize with it. Nevertheless, in my opinion she absolutely should not have any more children. I stressed that from my point of view it was imperative that they use absolutely sure birth-control measures. I said that I felt the risk was too great to depend on the rhythm system, which does not work for many couples, and that coitus interruptus was risky. I spelled out exactly what coitus interruptus was.

Her husband had been thoroughly scared for six months as he had seen his wife waver in and out of psychosis during her second illness, and he accepted my recommendation readily. He had broken away from the rigid Catholic upbringing of his youth. However, his wife was hesitant; she had gone directly from a convent school into marriage, and she saw her role in life as the mother of a brood of children whom she would lead triumphantly to heaven.

They used condoms for several months; she could not

bring herself to take contraceptive pills or to accept an intrauterine device. However, she was badly troubled. She confessed her sin each week to her priest, an elderly man who warned her to desist. Finally he spoke of the horrendous hell that for all eternity tortured with lightless fire the souls of those who rejected the teachings of God's church and persisted in carnal sin. She cried and pleaded with her husband; finally she refused to have sex with him anymore. The priest spoke to him. They began to use the rhythm system, and they stopped their periodic follow-up visits to me.

In time she got pregnant again, had the baby, and became psychotic once more. Again she was brought to St. Catharine's, but this time she was put under the care of a Catholic psychiatrist. During my daily rounds on the psychiatric ward at St. Catharine's I saw her occasionally in the dayroom or the corridor, and she always looked the other way. When I met Sister Margaret Dabney in the hospital admission office, we stuck to business and did not discuss her sister's illness.

Mrs. Kennedy was in and out of the St. Catharine's psychiatric ward for six months, and it was clear that things were not going well. For a while I didn't see her. Then, early one morning as I picked up the newspaper and glanced at it hurriedly before leaving home, I saw an old picture of her at the bottom of the first page under a headline; the picture must have been taken when she was in high school. When her husband had returned home the evening before, he had found the house locked and quiet. He had called a neighbor and had broken in. He had found his wife lying in the kitchen with a shotgun at her side; her face was unrecognizable. His three children had been similarly slaughtered in their beds. This had occurred about two weeks previous to today.

Sister Margaret Dabney came hurrying along the hall, her wide white skirts fluttering as she walked.

"It's very kind of you to see me, Doctor."

"I'm happy to do whatever I can, Sister." My words sounded awkward and silly to me.

She opened the door of the conference room and we went in. There was a long, heavy, polished table in the center, and dark wooden chairs lined its sides. The room was used mainly for committee sessions and board meetings. Pope Pius XII looked down at us from a time-dulled oil painting in an elaborate frame on the wall; his hand rested on a large gold cross on his chest.

Sister Margaret Dabney was tense and her face was wan. She looked somewhat like her sister, but she was much paler and thinner.

"Doctor," she said, "it's about Elizabeth. You know what happened, I guess."

"I saw it in the papers. I'm very sorry."

"Thank you, Doctor." She paused, obviously trying to find a way to go on. "Dr. Kane [her sister's psychiatrist at the time of her death] assures us that she was mentally ill and very disturbed when she died. She had a Christian burial. I'm sure she's at rest with God."

"Yes, she obviously was very sick," I said. "She didn't know what she was doing."

She picked up my words hurriedly. "Yes," she said, "she didn't know what she was doing. That's what I wanted to ask you."

I felt very ill at ease and, something that bothered me even more, perplexed; I did not understand what was going on. Sister Margaret Dabney obviously knew that her sister was mentally irresponsible when she murdered her children and killed herself. Hence, in Catholic theology she committed no sin when she performed these acts.

56

Something else was gnawing at Sister Margaret Dabney, and I did not see what it was.

After a moment of silence she went on. "To be frank, I trust you more than I trust Dr. Kane. Dr. Kane is a very good man and a fine doctor, but. . . ." She stopped altogether.

Then she started again. "You told us what could happen, but Dr. Kane just said that everything was all right and that she was doing fine. But he never really talked to her much, as you did."

The ensuing silence was difficult for both of us.

"Dr. Kane did his best, I'm sure," I said finally.

"Doctor," she said, "I want to know. It's very important to me. She said she was expecting a visit from the Holy Spirit and she felt that St. Anthony shook cups and rattled saucers in the cupboard and. . . . Well, was she really insane and absolutely not responsible for what she did?"

I replied, "She was insane, Sister. She was not responsible for what she did. I assure you of that. There is no doubt."

"And everything possible was done? Nothing could have been done differently? I think you know what I mean. It could not have been avoided in any way?"

I now saw the point of this interview. Sister Margaret Dabney was struggling to keep the fragments of her religion together. She had to believe that the deaths of her sister and the children were in no way related to the stupidity of an elderly Italian priest in Rome who had ruled that birth-control measures were against the law of God. To face the fact that her sister and the children had been sacrificed to the brutality of her religion was impossible for her. She was looking for a way out. She wanted me to tell her that the birth-control issue had no bearing whatsoever on this tragedy.

I lied to her. "It could not have been avoided. Even if she

had not got pregnant, she undoubtedly would have become insane again. I am sure. I saw her through two illnesses, and I knew her case well."

"Then the birth-control issue was really not important in the long run?"

I lied again. "No, in the long run it made no difference. It would have ended the same."

"Thank you, Doctor."

"It's okay, Sister." Idiotic words. It was not okay.

"I guess that's all, Doctor. You have been very kind. We have talked about you—the family, I mean. Perhaps she should have stayed with you."

"I am sure that even if she had stayed with me and even if she had followed my advice, it would have ended the same." This probably was a third lie.

She went to the door and opened it. Thanking me again and looking a little relieved, she bowed me out.

I wondered if she believed me. I think she did.

People usually believe what they must believe.

4

IT was 9:45 when I arrived on the psychiatric ward at St. Catharine's. As I walked into the nurses' station, Sister Mary Lawrence, the head nurse, said, "Sister Margaret Dabney would like to see you, Doctor." I replied that I had already spoken with her.

The ward secretary, who was temporarily out of the nurses' station, had stacked my seven charts on the doctor's table, and I sat down to look at them.

As I was reading through them, Ted Peters, who practices psychiatry in North Kansas City, came in.

"This is a crazy profession we're in," he said.

"ESP," I mumbled.

"Huh?"

"Extrasensory perception," I said. "I was just thinking the same thing."

He stared at me for a moment. I stared back and stifled a laugh. Ted Peters was a blunt man with a streak of eccentric righteousness in him. He wore his hair in a close-clipped crew cut and at unexpected times blurted out whatever happened to be on his mind.

"Give me five minutes of psychotherapy," he said.

I broke into laughter and was relieved to laugh. "Anytime," I answered. "And I won't charge you for it. Professional courtesy."

"I mean it," he said. "I'm a little shaken up."

"What's the matter?"

"I just came from Elmdale [a large private psychiatric hospital on the West Side of Kansas City]. I have a girl there. Thirty or so. Two kids. Husband works at the Chevrolet plant in Gladstone. First illness." When he is tense, Ted Peters spews out predicates, subjects, adjectives, and disconnected clauses higgledy-piggledy.

"Schizophrenia. Catatonic with deep regression. Lots of neologisms. A real word salad. And not chronic. Sick a couple of months. Early this morning I got a call from Elmsdale. The nurse said this girl just scratched her eyes out. I said, 'What do you mean, scratched her eyes out?' She said, 'Just that, scratched her eyes out.'"

"So I went over there and, sure enough, she did it."

"Did what?" I asked.

"She enucleated both her eyeballs at about five o'clock this morning. She just dug her thumbs in behind her eyes and pushed out her eyeballs. Ruptured both optic nerves and tore most of the muscles loose. They were both sort of hanging there when the nurse saw them."

"Good God," I muttered.

"They bandaged her up, and she's being transferred over here to St. Catharine's so she can be operated on. I called Elmer Wogan and he came over and saw her and said that of course both eyes must be removed. So she's coming over here by ambulance and they'll just complete the job and do some cosmetic repairs."

"It sounds awful," I said. "I know you must be pretty upset about it."

"I feel terrible," he replied. "And when I asked her why she did it, she just said, 'I scratched my eyes out.' Just repeated it. Nothing more. I had her on large doses of two antipsychotic medications and saw her every day. Since it

60

was her first illness, I thought maybe she wouldn't need shock. She never talked about scratching her eyes out or anything else like that. She has no history of ever having harmed herself in any way or of having tried to. You think I did everything possible for her, don't you?"

"Sure," I said. "This could happen to any of us. I'm just sorry that it happened to you. As they say, it couldn't happen to a nicer guy."

"It's funny," he said. "After this happened, her husband told me that her father shot himself in the garage one morning without a word of warning or a hint to anyone. They just went out and found him. And an uncle walked into the Missouri River one night for no reason anyone could give, and they fished him out at Jefferson City a few days later. Also, it seems she has an aunt, her mother's sister, who hasn't left her house in twelve years and won't say why. They didn't tell me all this until now. When she entered the hospital and I was taking her story and asked if there was any history of mental illness in the family, they said that none of them had ever been psychiatrically hospitalized. Which is so. They just go out and kill themselves or do other inexplicable things. A real weird family. In fact, her husband and her mother didn't seem particularly upset when I called them to the hospital this morning to tell them what had happened. I was much more upset than they were. Her mother actually seemed annoyed. She said that because she'd come to the hospital, she'd be late for work. A strange bunch of people. Sometimes I think there's something hereditary in all this. Maybe a screwed-up gene or a cracked chromosome or something."

"That would certainly let us off the hook," I said.

"Yeah. I was talking to a doctor from Sweden at the psychiatric convention in San Francisco last May. He said that over in Europe they look on this American jag on psychoanalysis and interpersonal relationships and all the rest of it as just one of those goofy things the Americans get tied up in once in a while, like Vietnam. Over in Sweden they think it's all mainly biochemical and constitutional —brain circuits out of whack and loused-up chromosomes; they say that environmental influences are just icing on the cake. He said that ninety percent of the psychiatrists over there think that our psychological theories are some wild tangent we've got onto. Except for little groups, they don't think much of Freud, either. They say he's a philosopher, not a scientist, and not a very good philosopher at that. Hell, I don't know. Anyway, that's what the Swede said."

He paused and muttered, "Just scratched her eyes out."

I put my hand on his shoulder. "Ted, it happens to us all. That's what we get paid for, to accept responsibility. Don't take it too hard. My father used to say that if you take life too seriously, it will drive you nuts."

"Thanks," he said, "I feel better."

"Well," I replied, "maybe there is something to psychological theory and therapeutic chitchat after all. Fifty-fifty, nature and nurture, constitution and environment, what you're born and what you're hit with. And it's a great life if you don't weaken. And I can't think of any more clichés to fit the occasion. Let me get at my charts. I have a few broken egos to repair today."

After I had been reading the nurses' notes and lab reports on my charts for a couple of minutes, the ward secretary came into the nurses' station and said, "Dr. Chapman, Dr. Powell called in early this morning. He's in bed with the flu and won't be making rounds until Wednesday. He said to ask you if you'd do the lumbar puncture on Miss Ryan for him. That way her workup will be finished by the middle of the week."

I said that I would and, turning to Sister Mary Lawrence, asked if the nurses were ready to do it.

62

"Yes, Doctor. Miss Rogowsky, one of the student nurses, will help you."

I looked around and saw Miss Rogowsky; her name was printed on the nameplate attached to her uniform. The one blue stripe on the small, peaked cap on the back of her head indicated that she was in the last year of nurses' training. She was a pleasant, round-faced girl, and what she lacked in beauty was made up for by the animal freshness and vitality that most adolescent girls have.

"Well, we might as well do the LP now," I said.

"Yes, Doctor," Miss Rogowsky replied. "I'll get the tray."

She went to a cabinet at the rear of the nurses' station, opened the metal door, and took out a large stainless-steel tray over which a thin white cloth was draped.

I frowned. "Are you absolutely sure that everything is there?" I asked sternly.

"Yes," said Miss Rogowsky, a little puzzled and startled by my tone.

"Good," I said, "I hate to give Communion and find something missing."

My joke went over well. Miss Rogowsky grinned, the ward secretary and Ted Peters guffawed, and Sister smiled broadly.

I went out the door, followed by Miss Rogowsky with her tray, and we entered Miss Ryan's room, a short distance down the hall. Miss Rogowsky placed the tray on a waist-high, metal, wheeled surgical cart that was already in the room; it had a bottle of alcohol, a bottle of Merthiolate, and a plastic slop basin on its lower tier.

"Perhaps you might get an aide to help us hold Miss Ryan in position," I said to Miss Rogowsky.

"Yes, Doctor." And she disappeared.

I turned to Miss Ryan. She was a fifty-seven-year-old single woman who was sitting on the edge of one of the two beds in the room, and she was dressed in a knee-length white surgical gown that was tied by strings in the back. She looked at me in an apprehensive, perplexed way and tensely rubbed her hands together.

"Good morning, Miss Ryan."

"Good morning, Doctor."

She paused. "You're not Dr. Powell."

"No, no, I'm Dr. Chapman. I'm the one who saw you first, in my office, before you came to the hospital."

"Oh, yes," she replied, embarrassed not to remember.

I helped her out. "There are so many doctors and nurses running in and out of here that you can't remember them all. It's not like the old days, when you had only one doctor to cope with."

She smiled weakly and looked anxiously at the tray and the surgical cart.

"Oh, that," I said. "Dr. Powell has a touch of the flu and won't be around this morning. He called in and asked me to do this little chore for him. However, he'll be as good as new by Wednesday, and then he'll go over the results of all your tests, tell us exactly what's wrong with you, and do whatever is needed to get you feeling all right again."

That was a lie. Miss Ryan was dying.

Miss Rogowsky had returned with a thin young man in a white uniform. I noted his name on the nameplate fastened to his jacket: Mr. Sowers. From that point on, I kept up a continual stream of soft, reassuring chatter. If we were to do our task easily, we needed a fully cooperative patient who would remain absolutely motionless in an awkward position for ten minutes. This can be a problem with a frightened, puzzled woman who doesn't grasp all that is going on around her. A pauseless flow of gentle, soothing talk is essential. What one says is not important, and it can be endlessly repetitive, but it must not falter if the patient is to stay calm. During military service I did more than two

64

hundred lumbar punctures, but I do only several a year now. My chatter during a lumbar puncture resembles, I'm afraid, the melodramatic, gooey way many people talk to children, but I've never found another way to do it.

"All right. I think we're ready. Good. Miss Rogowsky, you have all the things ready on the tray, and Mr. Sowers, you're ready. Now, Miss Ryan, this is just one of those routine tests we frequently do. It won't hurt any more than a pinprick, a mosquito bite, or one of those jabs in the arm when they take blood. And you've had plenty of those here in the hospital. Now, just lie down on the bed, on your side, with your face away from me and your back toward me. That's right. Will you go to the other side of the bed, Mr. Sowers? We'll need you there in just a minute. Fine. Now, Miss Ryan, slide back over toward the edge of the bed here, so that your back is even with the edge of the bed. That's it. Now, let's make sure that one hip is exactly above the other. Right. Now, bend your head forward on your chest. Down farther. That's fine. I know it's uncomfortable, but it will be for only a few minutes. Mr. Sowers will help you hold your head steady. Put your left hand here on the back of Miss Ryan's neck, Mr. Sowers. Good. Both of you hold steady. Now, Miss Ryan, double your knees up toward your stomach, like this. I'll straighten your gown. One knee exactly over the other and doubled up. Just like that. Okay. I'll position your back so that it's exactly straight up and down on the edge of the bed. Put your other hand right here to steady Miss Ryan's knees, Mr. Sowers. You're to help her not move a bit while we're doing the test. Good. I know that's a little awkward, Miss Ryan. However, if you can hold absolutely still in this position for five minutes, we'll have it all done."

The exact position of the patient is important if this procedure is to be done easily.

I untied the strings on Miss Ryan's gown, tucked the bottom half of the gown between her lower flank and the mattress, and doubled back the top half over her upper side; her back lay bare from her shoulders to the thin elastic band at the top of her underpants. While continuing my soft patter, I turned to the tray on the surgical cart. I removed the thin towel covering the tray and then untied the two cloth-wrapped packets and folded back the four flaps of each of them in such a way that their sterile contents lay exposed but uncontaminated. I glanced over the needles, syringes, ampules, tubes, and other items to make sure everything was there. Once in a while Central Supply leaves something out, and halfway through the procedure you find that you're stymied for lack of a minor piece of equipment. Everything was there.

"All right. Everything is on the tray, just as it should be. So, we'll get started, and in a few minutes we'll be finished. Then, after you rest in bed for a while, Miss Ryan, you'll be out in the dayroom watching television. I'll describe everything to you as we go along, Miss Ryan, so you won't be apprehensive about what's happening. First, the powder for my hands so the gloves will slip on easily. Now the gloves. The first one. Now the second one. Smooth out the wrinkles in them. Okay. Now, Miss Rogowsky, pour a little alcohol, please, on this cotton fluff at the end of my forceps. Good. Miss Ryan, you're going to feel a little cool fluid as I clean off a small part of your lower back with alcohol. It'll feel a little cool, but don't let that startle you, and don't move. Until I tell you about it first , nothing will hurt, and then it will be no more than a little needle jab. We have other things to do first. Now we're cleaning off the same small area of your back with Merthiolate. It feels the same, but it's not as cool. Now I'm going to put this large green drape over your back and side. Fine. Pull the top flap down

66

over your side, Mr. Sowers. Okay. This drape has a hole in it about the size of a lemon, right in the middle of the area I cleaned off with the alcohol and Merthiolate. That's the place where you'll feel the pinprick, but I'll tell you about it before it occurs. Now I'm getting a little Novocain out of an ampule and I'm putting it into a small syringe. Okay. I'm going to inject the Novocain into your skin down here at the lower end of your back. It's the same anesthetic the dentist injects before he drills. You're going to feel a pinprick right here where I'm pressing with my finger. Right . . . now. Fine. You didn't budge at all. I'm injecting the Novocain down into the skin and the tissues underneath it. You may feel a few more tiny jabs as I inject the Novocain deeper. Or you may not feel any more jabs, since I'm injecting the Novocain continually as I push the needle in. You're a very good patient. She didn't move at all, did she, Miss Rogowsky? All right. The Novocain needle is out."

This chatter may sound a little silly, but if you try sometime to maintain a flow of pauseless, reassuring talk while concentrating on an exacting mechanical procedure, you may feel more charitable toward me. The smoothness of the patter often determines whether this procedure is brief and almost painless or prolonged and agonizing. As an intern, before my chatter had been developed to its present level, I once spent an hour jabbing a screaming man held down by four aides, and when I finally got some spinal fluid out it was so bloody that it was useless for laboratory tests.

I next took a needle three inches long from the tray. It had a thin, removable bore occupying the entire length of its fine, hollow tube; the bore would be withdrawn after the needle had entered the spinal canal, allowing spinal fluid to flow out through the needle. While I was doing a lumbar puncture many years ago, an inexperienced aide, upon

67

seeing the three-inch needle, exclaimed, "Good God, Doctor, you don't intend to stick that thing into him, do you?" Needless to say, we had a difficult time on that occasion.

I carefully palpated the area that was exposed through the opening in the drape and felt the two bony knobs that lay beneath the skin. The upper one was the tip of the fourth lumbar vertebra and the lower one was the tip of the fifth lumbar vertebra. I placed the tip of the three-inch needle directly in the midline between the two vertebra, but somewhat closer to the fifth vertebra than the fourth one. As my chatter rippled on, I concentrated on the exact positioning of the needle. I lowered my eyes to its level to make sure it was entering on a precisely horizontal plane. If the needle deviated even slightly from the horizontal plane it would not reach its mark. Then I pushed the needle in, directing it slightly upward toward the fourth vertebra. It scraped on bone a couple of times as it gradually sank deeper, and on each occasion I directed it somewhat more in the direction of the fourth vertebra, always keeping it on a horizontal plane. About two inches of the needle were now in. It had reached the point where the Novocain stopped.

"Now, Miss Ryan, you're going to feel a pinprick, somewhat deep inside, and perhaps just a brief pinch of pain in one of your legs. Don't be afraid. It will be almost nothing at all and it will last as long as it takes to blink your eye." I then pushed the needle quickly inward until it met a firm resistance. I rapidly pushed it through that resistance and felt it slip a quarter of an inch farther. Miss Ryan gave a slight gasp of pain, and she moved slightly.

"I think that's it," I said reassuringly. "Just let me check to be sure. If the needle is where it should be, there won't be any more pain. You'll just hold this position for three

68

minutes and we'll be done." I pulled out the bore of the needle, and after a couple of seconds small drops of clear fluid began to drip from its opening. I replaced the bore to stop the flow of spinal fluid.

"Fine. We're in. In the next two to three minutes we'll simply measure the pressure of this fluid and collect a little of it to send to the laboratory. Hold absolutely steady and there will be no more pain, not even a pinprick."

I took a three-way stopcock from the tray, pulled out the bore of the needle, and fastened the stopcock securely on the end of the needle. I then took a fifteen-inch-long calibrated, hollow tube off the tray and fitted it onto the upper of the three outlets of the stopcock. I twisted the knob on the stopcock so that the fluid began to flow upward into the tube. It stopped after a few seconds, and I read the figure: 105. Following my instructions, Miss Rogowsky put one of her hands under Miss Ryan's neck and the other one over it. She briefly compressed the neck veins on one side, and then on the other side, and then on both sides. On the last occasion the fluid in the tube rose quickly and fell back to its former level when the pressure was released. I then twisted the knob on the stopcock to allow fluid to drip out of its downward spout; I let about a tablespoon of fluid drip into each of three small test tubes, which I corked and placed in a rack on the tray. I then measured the fluid pressure again in the calibrated tube and, with one fast jerk, pulled out the needle. A few drops of blood oozed from the puncture site. I wiped the blood off with a fluff of cotton and placed a Band-Aid over the puncture point.

Throughout the procedure my ceaseless prattle rolled on.

"That's all there is to it, Miss Ryan. Now, that wasn't too much, was it? Thank you, Mr. Sowers. Miss Rogowsky, perhaps you might take the drape off and tie the strings on

Miss Ryan's gown. Okay, now help her lie back in the center of the bed with her head flat. No pillow. In an hour or so, Miss Ryan, you can get up and go to the dayroom. If you got up right now, you might get a slight headache later on. Everything in the test worked out fine. The pressure measurements were completely normal. I'll take these three test tubes down to the nurses' station, and the ward secretary will send them off to the lab for a few tests."

I looked at Miss Rogowsky with feigned severity. "I never let nurses carry these tubes," I said. "Years ago we had a student nurse who stumbled and broke LP test tubes. The doctor strangled her on the spot, and he was acquitted on grounds of justifiable homicide. We wouldn't want that to happen to a pretty young girl like you, would we, Miss Rogowsky? Especially with the nursing shortage the way it is."

Miss Rogowsky grinned and Miss Ryan gave a pallid smile. I have a weakness for student nurses. Many of the girls I dated were student nurses, and my first sexual experiences were with them. Almost twenty-five years ago I married a nurse.

"In a couple of days or so, Miss Ryan, the results of all your tests will be back from the various labs. Then Dr. Powell will decide what kind of pills or shots to give you, and in a short time he'll have you back keeping the accounting department of the Santa Fe Railroad in good shape."

"Thank you, Doctor," she said.

Medical ethics require that when we lie to the patient we tell the family the truth.

I took the test tubes to the nurses' station, where the ward secretary labeled them and filled out lab requisition slips. She then gave them to an aide to take to the laboratory. I recorded the pressure readings in a progress note in Miss Ryan's chart.

70

Psychiatry is, by definition, a *medical* specialty, and therapists who forget it are in for some unpleasant surprises. I recall a consultation I did on a forty-four-year-old businessman who, after a year of psychotherapy for anxiety states and depressiveness, developed a slight weakness in his right upper eyelid; he died five months later of a brain tumor. I remember a woman who had two years of intensive psychotherapy as an inpatient at one of America's most prestigious psychiatric hospitals; a few months after she came back to Kansas City, still very sick, an electroencephalogram revealed unquestionable petit mal epilepsy, which had for two years been called "emotional blocking." I hope someday to forget a man whom I diagnosed as hysterical and whom I urged to go back to work while we explored his emotional problems in psychotherapy; autopsy eight months later showed widespread collagen disease, affecting his brain and spinal cord. I recall a woman who had extensive psychotherapy for what were felt to be her psychosomatic gastrointestinal problems until her cancer of the pancreas, from which she later died, became obvious. This melancholy recital of the errors of my colleagues and myself could be continued considerably, but I think I have made my point. So, all you psychologists, social workers, clergymen, and other aspirant therapists who want to get into the act, take care! It's more complicated than you think. The term "rap sessions" does not cover the subject.

Miss Ryan's mother had died seven months previously, and Miss Ryan, who except for brief periods had never lived separately from her mother, was desolate. She sank into a depressed, agitated state that grew steadily worse. Until her mother's death Miss Ryan had been a shy, pleasant person, dedicated to her mother, her church, and her job; for thirty-five years she had worked in the accounting division of the Santa Fe Railroad. Her brothers

71

sent her for a two-month vacation with a married sister in Arizona. She returned from Arizona unimproved, and six weeks before the day of her lumbar puncture, her family physician sent her to me.

At first glance she looked like a passive, dependent woman who had been able to make a reasonably good adjustment while she had her mother to lean on and had deteriorated badly after her mother's death. But she didn't smell right. It is neither elegant nor scientific to say that a patient doesn't smell right, but after you've been wading knee-deep in the variegated forms of human misery for two or three decades you begin to develop intuitive perceptions about patients. There was something about Miss Ryan that didn't fit.

Perhaps it was an aimless distractibility in her manner, or her occasional difficulty in remembering minor things, or ever so slight a hint of disarray in the way she strung her sentences together. At the beginning of my third session with her I pulled a black, oblong leather kit off the shelf of my bookcase and went through the essential points in a neurological examination on her. When I ran the tip of the handle of my reflex hammer up the outer side of the sole and across the ball of her left foot, her big toe turned upward instead of downward, as it should have done, and her toes fanned outward instead of inward, as would be expected. This is called a positive Babinski. It was the only abnormality in the examination, but it was enough.

I told her that I thought she was merely upset over her mother's death, but that she should go to St. Catharine's Hospital to have a few tests to make sure we weren't overlooking any physical difficulty that "might be contributing to the problem," and that we'd have Dr. Powell, a neurologist, take a look at her. She was admitted to a general medical floor under Dr. Powell, but one night she became confused and wandered down the hall. Hospital stairs have metal-tipped steps, and so Miss Ryan was transferred to the psychiatric ward, where her neurological workup continued.

The results of her examinations are almost all in, and it is clear that she has a rapidly spreading degenerative disease of the brain. Dr. Powell says she is an interesting case. She will be dead within a year.

After checking the nurses' notes and the order sheet in Miss Ryan's chart, I finished reading the nurses' notes in my other charts and turned to Sister Mary Lawrence.

"How is Mrs. Underwood coming along, Sister?"

She laughed. "She has short lucid intervals at times, but she lapses back. Yesterday she recognized Father Ritter when he came to visit her, but when he left, she called him Monsignor O'Brien. And several times a day she still wants to take the student nurses out into the garden to show them her prize peonies. However, she's improving slowly. In another couple of weeks we may be able to start her in OT. We're using her as a teaching case. She's the first Korsakov's psychosis we've had in two years."

Mrs. Underwood was a fifty-five-year-old woman who had been a chronic alcoholic for twenty-five years. She drank wine alone at home. She was a prominent Catholic laywoman who knew or was related to everybody of any prominence in Catholic social circles in Kansas City. About three weeks previously she had lapsed into a Korsakov's psychosis, a rare type of alcoholic brain disorder in which the patient has a severe loss of memory that he covers with elaborate fictional tales. Thus, Mrs. Underwood each day described to the nursing staff and other patients all the details of the cocktail parties, luncheons, and banquets that she stated she had attended the day before, and she embellished her stories with the names of Kansas City's social elite. One day the Bishop of Kansas City paid her a brief visit on the ward and caused quite a stir. After that the student nurses were never quite sure what was fact and what was fabrication in her tales.

Patients with Korsakov's psychosis almost invariably get well in a couple of months if they are given good nursing care and large doses of vitamin B complex. Gay, charming Mrs. Underwood was a ward pet, and anecdotes grew up thickly around her.

After she recovered from her Korsakov's psychosis, I got to know Mrs. Underwood well. Unlike most patients who have had an alcoholic psychosis, she never drank again. Also, she came to see me every ten days or so for the next year. She never said why she came, but I think it was because she felt that I was the only one who knew her story. There was, I guess, some comfort to her in our shared secrets.

She was reared on a ranch in Idaho, a wild, free tomboy. Her mother died when she was six, and her father let her do as she wished. When she was nineteen, John Underwood came to the small Idaho town near her father's ranch. He was the only son of a wealthy Kansas City mortgage broker, and until he was twenty-one he had been completely dominated by his parents. Then he grabbed what money he had and broke away. He went to Idaho, where he bought a ten-gallon hat and lounged in the bars. Somehow he met Rosalyn McCord. She took him for a dashing Kansas City man of the world and fell in love with him. They married and lived in Idaho on her father's ranch for two years. When her father died and his debts swallowed his estate, John and Rosalyn returned, penniless, to Kansas City.

John Underwood's burst of brave rebellion was brief. When he returned to Kansas City, he fell back into his old pattern of dutiful submission to his domineering parents, and he became a minor employee at a modest salary in his father's firm. His parents made all their decisions for them and kept them on a cruelly tight financial rein. They spent each Sunday at his parents' home and dined there every Wednesday night. John's parents both lived into their middle eighties, and when, two years before I treated her, their wealth finally came to John and Rosalyn, it no longer meant anything to her.

Over a several-year period after coming to Kansas City, Rosalyn slowly perceived that her dashing prince was really a timid little boy, afraid of his parents and completely dependent on them emotionally and financially. She turned to her children. The first was a girl and the second was a boy; she had no more. The girl died in an automobile accident when she was eight and Rosalyn was thirty. With her death a dull depressiveness settled on Rosalyn, but it was hidden by solitary alcoholism at home and a façade of social gaiety outside it.

Divorce was impossible. Her religion and her feelings for her son were too strong for that. But they did not prevent her from taking a lover, and a most unlikely one at that. Her parish priest. They were lovers for twenty-five years, and though some suspected, no one was sure. As middle age crept upon Rosalyn and old age came to the priest, the terror and guilt of both of them were severe, since they believed in the eternal hell that waited for them beneath their feet. She blanketed her fear in ever severer alcoholism. By the time she developed her Korsakov's psychosis she had become a haggard, bewildered wreck shambling around her house.

While she was in the hospital, the priest, in his middle sixties, died suddenly of a heart attack. I think his death was the main reason she stopped drinking. With him they

75

buried her sin and guilt. Six months after she stopped coming to see me Mrs. Underwood followed him. I hope their religion is false, and they are not where they feared they would go.

I went down my list of patients and did my tasks.

I talked with Mrs. Underwood and made sure she was getting the medications she needed.

I gave Mr. Hagan his electroshock treatment. Mr. Hagan was a sheet-metal worker from Liberty, Missouri, who once every two to three years had a manic psychosis. Antipsychotic drugs, lithium medication, and psychotherapy did not work on him, but five or six electroshock treatments did the trick in less than three weeks. His manic episodes were so regular that periodically Sister Mary Lawrence would say, "It's about time for Mr. Hagan to come in again, isn't it, Doctor?" and he usually did. Some psychiatrists decry electroshock, and it *is* terribly abused by lazy and unscrupulous psychiatrists, but it also is the only thing that works on some patients. You give the patients what they need, and the theories come tumbling after.

Mrs. Spinelli was a schizophrenic who was about ready to go home. I chatted with her for ten minutes and stressed that after leaving the hospital she must continue her medication and keep her follow-up appointments with me.

When I was a medical student, the prognosis of schizophrenia, the most common psychotic illness, was ghastly. The vast majority of the patients slowly deteriorated into permanent incapacitation and gibbering delusional states. About that time electroshock became the main form of treatment, and the prognosis improved somewhat. In the early 1950's a French pharmaceutical firm put out a new medication to improve the efficiency of anesthetics during surgical operations; it was called chlorpromazine. About

76

the same time, both in America and Europe, it was accidentally discovered that this preanesthetic drug had a phenomenal impact on schizophrenics. When it was given in large doses, the vast majority of schizophrenics got well in from one to four months, and most of them stayed well if they remained on small maintenance doses of the drug for several years more.

This precipitated a frenzy of research in American and European pharmaceutical laboratories, and the 1950's saw the introduction not only of many effective drugs for schizophrenia but also, for the first time, truly effective drugs for about two-thirds of depressed patients. Since 1954, despite constantly rising admission rates, the population of American psychiatric hospitals has declined each year. No real advances in psychotherapy or indeed in psychological theories have occurred since the late 1940's. Old theories are polished up a bit or are resurrected to enjoy new waves of enthusiasm and are hailed by their proponents as epochal. The public is titillated by these alleged discoveries. But the major change in psychiatry since 1950 has been the pharmacologic revolution of which Mrs. Spinelli is a beneficiary.

And nobody knows how or why any of these medications works. The physician who needs a theory to prop him up can choose one of the dozen or so that are available, but if he wishes to hold tightly to his theory, he had better not examine the evidence too closely.

So far, the 1970's have produced no basic advances in psychiatric treatment; we are in a lull. Medical progress usually comes in surges; the dam bursts and the waters rush on until they meet the next obstacle. Better delivery of psychiatric services to the public is perhaps occurring, but the treatment techniques themselves are not improving.

After leaving Mrs. Spinelli, I spent some time talking

with the nurses and aides about the management of Mr. Tapp, a senile seventy-six-year-old man who was hospitalized briefly on his way from his apartment to a nursing home. The apartment-building manager had demanded that Mr. Tapp's married daughter take him from the building after he was found wandering naked in the hall one night. We were not supposed to hospitalize untreatable senile patients on the psychiatric ward of St. Catharine's, but Mr. Tapp's son-in-law was a physician on the staff, and the administration winked its eyes when I promised that he would be there no more than ten days.

The next patient was Norma Overton, a nineteen-year-old, five-months pregnant mentally retarded girl with an IQ of 60. I had first seen her when she was twelve and had attempted to counsel her parents about her special needs and problems. However, her mother had refused to accept the fact that Norma was retarded: "A little slow perhaps, but not retarded." Her mother pressured the teachers in the small suburban school Norma attended to keep her in regular classes and to pass her along from grade to grade despite her failure to master the material; since she was docile enough at that time, the teachers went along with the mother's urging. I saw Norma again when she was sixteen. By this time sex had become a problem; she was an easy mark for the boys who ran after her. I pressed her mother strongly to obtain legal guardianship over her and to place her in a state school for mentally retarded adolescents. Her father had long ago abandoned any attempt to struggle with his wife over Norma. The mother still refused to accept Norma's retardation and said that all Norma needed was some guidance about her relationships with boys.

By the time she entered St. Catharine's she had become unmanageable. She often stayed out all night, and her belly had grown until her lies about not being pregnant were no longer tenable. Her mother finally had accepted her daugher's retardation, and Norma, genial and cooperative enough in the hospital, was awaiting transfer to a state institution where she would have her baby; afterward it would be put up for adoption. Her parents had initiated proceedings in the county court to obtain guardianship over her. A special court hearing declaring a person incompetent and giving another individual full authority over him is necessary to protect a girl like Norma from exploitation by unscrupulous persons. I filled out the necessary papers and would have to testify at the court hearing, where a state-appointed attorney would represent Norma to see that her best interests were served.

A psychiatrist has to know a certain amount of law.

The last patient was Joan Guthrie, a woman in her middle twenties, whom I found sitting in a chair in a corner of her room. She did not look up as I entered and gave no sign of awareness that I was there during the five minutes I spent with her. She was resting her elbows on the arms of her chair and was staring intently at her hands, which she held directly in front of her face about twelve inches from her eyes. The fingers of each hand were tightly pressed together, and she held her left hand flat under her right one in a horizontal plane, as if they were two thin boards lying one on top of the other. The tips of the fingers of the top hand rested on the knuckles of the lower one. The ends of her thumbs touched lightly in the midline, on a level a little below that of her layered fingers. About once every ten seconds Joan separated the tips of her thumbs slightly for a second or two, without moving her fingers, and then joined the tips of her thumbs together again. Except for the time she had spent sleeping, eating, bathing, going to the toilet, and attending to other basic necessities, Joan had been doing this for most of her life. When I first saw her, she was two years and eleven months old, and she already had begun to spend much time engaged in this activity.

Joan is one of identical twins; her sister's name is Jean. I first examined Joan and Jean in the psychiatric clinic of a children's hospital at which I spent one afternoon each week doing consultations and teaching medical students. The parents of Joan and Jean had brought them to the hospital's ear-nose-and-throat clinic because they thought the girls might be deaf.

Their parents had first noticed abnormalities in these girls during the latter months of their first year of life. They were apathetic and indifferent to the attentions of the parents and other adults who cared for them. They were physically less active than most infants; they lay motionless for long periods of time. During their second and third years they were somewhat slower than other children in learning to sit, stand, and walk. However, their most striking abnormality was their muteness. Although both of them occasionally uttered guttural noises and low moans, they were silent most of the time. Toward the end of the third year of life Jean learned to say "mama," but Joan said no words at all. In addition, they did not play with other children or with each other. If one of them accidentally interfered with an activity of the other, they both became agitated, thrashed their arms about, and moved apart.

When I examined them in front of several medical students, with their parents looking on, each of the twins at first wandered about the examination room in a purposeless way, paying no attention to anyone. Joan soon stopped in a corner, facing a wall; she placed her hands before her face in her characteristic two-tiered way, stared at them, and moved no more. About the same time Jean began to walk in a small circle, grunting low in a rhythmic way and stamping her right foot at every fourth step; she held her arms slightly apart from her body and let them hang down limply.

After watching them for a few minutes, I went to the corner where Joan was standing and I abruptly shrieked in her ear; she did not appear startled or in any other way indicate that she had heard anything. Jean remained similarly unresponsive to a sudden shout behind her. However, when a secretary began to type in an adjacent office Jean abruptly stopped her rhythmic movements for a few seconds and Joan cocked her head backward. I sent one of the medical students to tell the secretary to stop typing for two minutes and then to begin again. The girls reacted in the same manner when the typing once more commenced. The sound of a door opening and shutting in an outside office had a similar effect on them.

Joan's behavior has remained much the same since the first day I saw her. She has never said a word, and except for dressing herself, eating, and carrying out the other simple activities that are necessary for survival, she has spent her life looking raptly at her hands. She does it in all situations and in all postures.

Jean has developed quite differently. She gradually learned to talk and by the age of eight could express her needs and feelings fairly well. However, until she was five she could not use the pronouns "I" and "you" accurately; it was as if her relationships between people were so confused that she had trouble distinguishing between herself and other people. She also did not learn the word "yes" until she was five years old, though she learned to say "no" at the age of three. Until the age of about eight or nine Jean had a strong preoccupation with maintaining the sameness of everything in her environment. For example, if the position of a chair or a small rug or a lamp in her bedroom was changed by even a few inches, she became very agitated and worked frantically to get it back to its precise original place.

In contrast to her grossly impaired contacts with *people* during her childhood, Jean had an intense interest in *things*. For hours at a time she would earnestly study the details of a picture in a children's book, and wallpaper designs fascinated her. She had repetitive games that she played for long periods. In one of them she set a dozen pencils or crayons on a slightly inclined plane, such as a board or a thin book, tilted downward toward herself. She removed the bottom pencil or crayon and placed it at the top of the stack, letting the others roll down the inclined surface; her absorption in this ritual was intense, and if her mother took away her pencils or crayons she groaned desolately for an hour or two.

In later childhood Jean began to interact more with people. She talked more, but in an odd, lilting cadence. Between the ages of seven and ten she could recite verbatim fifty- to one-hundred-line poems and whole pages of children's books that had been read to her two or three times, and she could hum or sing several-minute stretches of popular and light classical music that she had heard a few times on her father's stereo set. These memory feats were not signs of superior intelligence; they were merely one more aspect of her continuing preoccupations with things as opposed to people.

During adolescence Jean steadily improved. She completed grade school at fifteen and finished high school at nineteen. She remained a shy, quiet girl and she never dated. Her parents attempted to have her attend a small liberal arts college while living at home, but on each of three trials she panicked and balked. In her early twenties she became a typist in an office of the telephone company, where her father is a departmental manager; in high school

82

she had learned typing and routine office procedures. She goes to work and returns home each day with her father.

Thus, Jean's development has been quite different from that of Joan, who has spent her life looking at her hands at home. They have an older sister and a younger brother whose development has been normal.

Joan and Jean are identical twins. That is, they developed from the same fertilized egg that separated into two identical parts in its first division. Hence, in all biological respects they are completely similar. Identical twins are contrasted with fraternal twins, who develop from two separate eggs that happen to be fertilized by two different spermatozoa about the same time. Fraternal twins are no more alike than brothers or sisters who are born at separate times, and they may, of course, be of opposite sexes.

After studying Joan and Jean for several months, I reported their case in a psychiatric journal (*Archives of Neurology and Psychiatry,* Volume 78, December, 1957). It was the third report in the medical literature of this condition in identical twins. A few months after that article was published, a medical research foundation on the East Coast contacted me and offered to furnish the necessary money each year to follow these girls as long as I could, with yearly psychological examinations, psychiatric observations, neurological workups, and biochemical studies. This research foundation is now following about two hundred cases of this type of disorder in twins, with long-term data on them. For unclear reasons 90 percent of the cases are identical twins. Joan was now in St. Catharine's for her once-yearly battery of studies. Jean had had hers on an outpatient basis.

During their childhood and early adolescence, repeated attempts were made to treat each of these girls in child-guidance clinics, but no therapist was able to form a relationship with either one; each girl remained silent and immobile during her treatment sessions. Even after she had improved socially, Jean resisted each therapist's overtures. Over the years, at the request of the medical research foundation, each girl had trials of three to six months on several kinds of antipsychotic medications, but these drugs had no beneficial effects. When they were eleven, a psychiatrist who was serving for a year as consultant to the research foundation wanted me to give them electroshock treatment, but I refused.

What is wrong with Joan and Jean? We have a name for it, of course. It is called early infantile autism, and it was first described in the middle 1940's. Until that time these children had been diagnosed as mentally retarded or deaf-mute or brain-damaged. Although labeling their troubles doesn't help patients much, it aids physicians in thinking and talking more clearly about them. To be brief, we don't know what causes this type of disorder, and we can only speculate about why Joan has remained fixed in her state of profound emotional withdrawal while Jean has to a large extent emerged from it. If the causes of this disorder are interpersonal, there should be more evidence of highly damaging relationships with parents and other close persons during the child's earliest months of life; however, in many cases, including that of Joan and Jean, exhaustive studies reveal little evidence of emotional stress or not enough to explain so severe a disturbance. If the causes lie in biochemical abnormalities or defective genes, why has Joan remained so sick while Jean has made substantial progress?

Of every one hundred children with this condition, about seventy-five remain, like Joan, very withdrawn all their lives. Another twenty make the kind of partial "social recovery" that Jean has made. A final five of them recover entirely by the time they reach late adolescence or early adulthood. There is no treatment that affects the course of this disorder or alters the percentages of patients who improve or recover. Three decades of psychological, biochemical, neurological, and chromosomal research have yielded no reliable information about what is wrong with these patients.

I sat and watched Joan for five minutes while she stared at her hands. Abruptly, she became physically tense and her thumbs stopped their repetitive movements. I looked around the room to see if anything had happened, but everything seemed the same. I listened carefully for any new sound. After a few seconds I caught it. An airplane was flying over the hospital as it lowered to come into the Kansas City International Airport, which is about five miles from St. Catharine's Hospital. Its hum was soon gone, and Joan was again completely absorbed in studying her hands.

I rose and left the room.

5

IT was a little past 11:00. I went back to the nurses' station and wrote a few orders and progress notes. The telephone rang. The ward secretary answered it and handed it to me. It was the emergency room.

My stomach tightened. When a psychiatrist gets a call from an emergency room, it often means serious trouble. The most common trouble is a suicide or a suicidal attempt, sometimes with pills the psychiatrist prescribed for the patient.

"What's the problem?" I asked.

"There's a Mr. Farnsworth down here with his son. He wants to see you. He says it's urgent."

I relaxed. I knew socially a couple of Mr. Farnsworth's brothers. However, I had not treated anyone by that name. So I didn't have another suicide to chalk up on my blackest of boards.

"I'll be right down."

I left the ward and waited for an elevator, while a brown-robed statuette of St. Anthony holding the infant Jesus in his arms looked benevolently at me from a wall niche. I wondered what he would have thought about birth-control pills and Mrs. Kennedy's slaughter of her children and herself. I buzzed two or three times for the elevator, and finally it came.

I went down to the emergency room and looked around. There was the usual collection of patients there—a few people with wet casts on their ankles and wrists, an elderly woman on a stretcher waiting to be admitted, a man with a bandaged arm, a girl whose face was peppered with glass from a shattered automobile windshield, a badly wheezing asthmatic, and others. As I looked around, Paul Farnsworth got up from a bench in a corner and brought along a tall adolescent boy.

"Hello, Paul."

"Hello, Harry. This is my son Matthew."

"Hi, Matthew."

"Hi." He shifted from one foot to the other and glanced anxiously around the room; his hands fidgeted constantly.

Silence.

"I take it you have some problem, Paul?"

"Yes. Matthew has a problem. Is there somewhere we can talk alone?"

"The three of us?" I asked.

"Yes."

"Well, let me see."

I checked with the nurse in charge, who said that one of the treatment rooms was not being used. We went in. I lifted myself onto the table, with my legs dangling over the edge. I patted the table beside me and nodded to Matthew to sit at my side. His father sat down on a metal chair.

"What's the problem, Paul?"

"Matthew is in his junior year at Southwest. He's been an honor student every semester except the last one. He's always been a good boy. We've had our little problems with the other two, but we never had any trouble with Matthew."

This was the preamble, the apology. But it also gave some relevant information. If Matthew's adjustment had been fairly good until now, and he'd recently deteriorated in some way, the chance that I could get him back to his usual level of adjustment or that he would get there spontaneously, with or without my aid, was much better than if he had never had a good adjustment.

This is a general axiom in psychiatry. If the psychiatrist's problem is to return a patient to a good level of functioning that he long had but recently lost, he probably will get the job done. If, on the other hand, the problem is to create a level of adjustment the patient never had, the psychiatrist is much less likely to get the task done. In the long run, this tends to be true regardless of the kind of treatment the patient receives—intensive psychotherapy, flexible psychotherapy, medications, or electricity. Psychiatrists who disagree with this axiom are, in the main, those who see small, not-too-sick groups of patients or administrative or academic psychiatrists who have had relatively little long-term experience in working with patients.

Paul Farnsworth found it hard to go on.

"And now Matthew has a problem?" I asked.

"He's been taking drugs."

I turned to Matthew. "What kind of drugs have you been taking, pal?"

He glared at me with a look that told me not to call him "pal" anymore. The word "pal" was a mistake; my generation gap was showing. I should have said "man."

"Speed. That's all," he said sullenly.

I had the feeling that Matthew and I were going to be honest enemies.

"No acid?" I asked.

"That's for kids," he replied.

"Coke?"

"No. Well, only a little."

"A little" often means "a lot."

"Pot?"

"Everybody smokes a little pot now and then."

"Nothing else?" I asked.

"No." He pounded his right fist up and down softly on the pallet of the examining table and scowled at the floor. This consultation obviously was his father's idea and he wanted none of it.

"And why does all this happen to blow up right now, on a Monday morning?" I asked.

He waved his hand toward his father, and I looked at him.

"We couldn't get him out of bed for school this morning. He was groggy. We've suspected for a while, and so we went through his closet and drawers and found these."

He pulled out a small metal box with syringe needles, a syringe, an eye dropper, and a bent teaspoon. It also contained a small amount of white powder in a plastic sack. I spread these things out on the treatment table beside me while Matthew watched me nervously, and his father looked anguished and haggard.

"It's just a little speed," Matthew said. "That's all." He turned to his father. "Speed. That's amphetamine, what you take to lose weight."

Matthew's eyes met mine. I knew he was lying and he knew that I knew.

I opened the plastic sack, wet my finger on my tongue, touched it into the powder, and tasted it. Bitter. I wrapped up the powder, slipped the rubber band around the neck of the sack, rearranged the things in the kit, and snapped the metal lid back onto it.

"How long have you been using this stuff?" I asked.

"Not long. A few weeks." That usually means a few months or more.

"What stuff?" his father asked.

I did not answer.

"Let me see your arms," I said to Matthew.

He did not move, so I took his left wrist in my right hand and gently twisted the underside of his forearm upward. I pushed his sweater and shirt sleeve up to above his elbow.

He did not cooperate and he did not resist. I did the same thing to the other arm and held the two arms side by side before me. I rotated both arms slightly to one side and back so that the light would fall across their surfaces at somewhat different angles. I passed my fingertips up and down each forearm once or twice. There were little hard knots along the major veins, a few blue spots, and some older pink scars on his left arm. There were one or two fresh red points.

"Speed," Matthew said. "I pop it."

"Yeah," I said. He wasn't going down without a fight.

I took his face in my hands and turned it toward the light. Despite the fact that the room was brightly lighted his pupils were widely dilated. He shoved my hands away and stared at his knees. There was gooseflesh on his arms and he shifted from one ham to the other.

"I guess your last shot was about midnight?"

He looked at me belligerently and said nothing.

"What does all this mean?" his father asked. His voice was a little unsteady.

"Well," I replied, "I would say that it's about ninety-five percent sure that your boy is hooked on heroin and has been so for two to three months. He has all the signs."

"My God," his father said. "He's only fifteen."

"They start early these days," I said.

I turned to his son. "Matthew, I know you're not too enthusiastic about me just now, but I've been around, and I know a kid who's hooked on junk when I see one. You're going to be hospitalized here or somewhere else, and it'll be

90

a lot smoother for you if you fill me in. How long have you been hooked on this stuff?"

He was cornered. "A month or so. Maybe a little more."

His father was breathing shallowly and his face quivered slightly as he watched us.

"Where did you get the money?"

"I sold a few things." He paused. "I also lifted a few things from stores."

"And never got caught?"

"No."

"Lucky boy. Or maybe not so lucky," I said.

"Where did you get the stuff?" A useless question, but I threw it out. Just fishing.

"There's a kid who peddles it."

"Well, where do you go from here?" I asked.

That's an old psychiatrist's trick. Throw an impossible question at the patient to force him to agree with you. He obviously cannot say, "I want to go home and continue stealing and shooting heroin," though that is really what he wants to do.

Silence.

I turned to his father. "The best thing is to hospitalize him here on the psychiatric service. We'll take him off the stuff gradually over a ten-day period. Then we'll talk about money and go over the fine print in your hospitalization insurance policy where it deals with narcotic addiction. After that we'll choose the best place to send him for six months or more of rehabilitation and group psychotherapy."

"Six months?" his father gasped.

"At least that," I answered. "It takes that long or more to break his yearning for the stuff and his connection with whoever's selling it to him. We shall probably send him to the general adolescent division of the state psychiatric hospital at Fulton or Farmington. If he goes to a special ward for narcotic addiction at the federal or state hospital, he just spends his time talking to a lot of long-term addicts who probably will make him an addict for life."

"Why can't he just stay here at St. Catharine's?"

"How many other kids do you have, Paul?" I knew the answer, but I had a point to make.

"Two others."

"Then he can't stay here. The cost would be crushing and unfair to you, your wife, and the other two children. Even the best insurance policies cover a maximum of fifteen to thirty days on narcotic addiction. The people who write insurance policies read statistics, and when they read the statistics on the cure rates of narcotic addiction, they shift their benefits to other kinds of problems. Save your money for the education of your other two kids."

I corrected myself: "I mean, for all three kids."

I quite possibly was right the first time.

"Matthew will do as well at Fulton or Farmington as he would here at St. Catharine's during the six months' rehabilitation period."

I turned to Matthew, who was watching me with a slight mocking smile.

"You can't hold me against my will," he said. "So you might as well stop bluffing."

"A lawyer yet," I replied. "Matthew, your father said you're fifteen. When is your birthday?"

"December," his father answered. "December twenty-second."

"I was a Christmas present," Matthew said in a taunting way.

He was getting under my skin. The bare hostility of most addicts to their doctors makes it difficult for physicians to

92

keep their counterirritability under control. However, I've seen a lot of Matthews. So I relaxed, shifted my buttocks on the table, and went on.

"Matthew, you and I both know that you didn't want to come here today. But we also know that since you came I've got to do what I'm supposed to do, and so let's make the best of it." I paused.

"You're hooked on junk. You're fifteen and have almost ten months to go before you're sixteen. In this state your father can sign you in and out of any hospital, regardless of your wishes, until next December twenty-second. So settle down and it will be easier for all of us. We'll take you off the stuff as easily as we can. I'll snow you under with a tranquilizer during the hard part, a tranquilizer you can't get hooked on."

He snorted and tossed his head back.

"Suppose I don't want to stay for your little picnic? 'Stone walls do not a prison make/Nor iron bars' a something-or-other. . . .'" he said.

I laughed.

"A poet yet," I said. "Anyway, that's better than a lawyer, with all due respect to your father." Paul Farnsworth was a lawyer.

"Well, of course it's possible that you could get out of here, but it's unlikely. I'm not exactly an idiot, and I'll do my best to see that you don't. We'll give you medications that will keep you calm, maybe even a little drowsy, while you're here. We don't use straitjackets anymore. That's barbaric. We use what we call 'chemical restraint.' That's scientific."

"And what if I don't take your pills?" he said.

"Well, Matthew, I've been all through this a few times before. I've made my little mistakes and learned my little lessons. We don't give you pills. We give all your medications in liquid form. Besides, for the first ten days we mix the narcotic withdrawal substitute, methadone, and the tranquilizer in the same cocktail. To get the methadone, which you need to stop the horrors, you must take the other. The cocktail is given once every six hours while you're coming off the junk, and the nurses watch you take it and wash it down with a little water."

"Smart-ass medic, aren't you?" said Matthew.

"I have to be," I replied. "Some of my patients are very bright."

He laughed for the first time. Flattery *does* get you somewhere.

"But you can't keep me a zombie for six months on tranquilizers."

"A very bright boy," I said. "You can go to the head of the class. You're quite right. After two to three weeks we can't snow you under anymore, or at least there's no point in it. Then a smart boy like you can get out of wherever he is, if he really wants to. But where would you go? Home to Mother and Daddy?"

"I could make it on the street."

"And then one morning the cops would find the rats nibbling at your body after some teenage hood bashed in your skull in an alley to get whatever cash and dope you had on you. It happens every day."

For the first time he was a little frightened. This is what the books call "mobilizing anxiety in the patient." It perhaps would be more honest to call it "bullying the patient into treatment for his own good."

I turned to his father. "Do you go along with this, Paul?"

"I guess I have to," he replied.

"Stay here with him for a minute," I said.

I slipped Matthew's narcotics kit into my pocket (there was less chance of him trying to make a run for it if he was without his injection kit and his supply of heroin) and went out to the emergency-room office. I called the admission office and got a bed for him on the psychiatric floor. I then phoned medication orders and a little background information to the nurses on the psychiatric floor and asked them to send two male aides to the emergency room.

I went back to Matthew and his father. In a couple of minutes the aides came. Matthew parted sullenly from his father and started toward the door, arm-in-arm with one aide and flanked by the other. At the door he turned to me.

"What are you going to do with my kit and my junk?" he asked.

"I'll crush your kit under my heel and throw it in the nearest wastebasket. I'll flush the junk down the toilet. It's illegal to have it in my possession, you know."

"They're mine," he retorted.

"'Lead us not into temptation,'" I replied.

"A smart-ass medic," he said and went out with the aides.

His father looked at me blankly for a few seconds and said, "What will happen to him?"

"He'll be all right. No visitors for two weeks. It's better that way. Then you, your wife, and I will get together in my office and make long-range hospitalization plans for him. In the meantime, you check your insurance policy to see what it covers. Right now I'll take you to the admission office to sign the admission papers and give them the other data they need. They'll tell you what to bring him later today—clothes, toothbrush, and so forth."

"That's not what I mean," his father said. "What will happen to him in the long run? Where will he be a year from now, two years from now, five years from now?"

That was the question I didn't want him to ask.

"Well, he's young. He's been taking the stuff a relatively short time. His outlook is a lot better than that of most addicts. Underneath all that hostility I get the feeling that he's a good, sound kid. He has a good chance of making it. Tell his mother that, and tell her to make an appointment to see me personally if she wants to hear it directly from me." This was not my honest opinion of Matthew's probable future, and I was offering to tell the same fibs to his mother.

His father looked a little relieved. It was like giving aspirin to a man with a brain hemorrhage and telling him he'd be all right. Of course, there was a 10 to 20 percent chance that the boy eventually would stop taking heroin, and these percentages were much better than those of the average older addict. However, discussing percentage figures with his parents would only rob them of a few years of greater hope.

I took Paul Farnsworth to the admission office, and there we parted. He was a badly shaken man. I thought of my own children, of the dangers that the future perhaps held for them, and all the horrors that lurked in the streets. It was so different when I was Matthew's age in the 1930's.

I went back to the emergency room, picked up one of the phones that was connected with the tape recorders in the central typing pool, and dictated an admission note on Matthew. I then phoned the psychiatric ward and asked if Sister Mary Lawrence was there. She was. I asked to speak to her.

"This is Dr. Chapman, Sister. The Farnsworth boy who just arrived up there is addicted to heroin, but he won't give any big problems."

"The administration doesn't like us to admit addicts, Doctor. They usually sign out against advice in a couple of days and cause a great deal of trouble."

96

"I know, Sister. That's why I'm calling you. This boy comes from an old Kansas City family. His grandfather was one of the first reform councilmen when they threw out the Pendergast machine in 1940. I went to grade school with his father and his uncle. The boy is fifteen and has almost ten months to go before he's sixteen. So with his father's signature we can hold him. Also, I've given him heavy, flexible chlorpromazine orders. You can use up to six hundred milligrams every twelve hours if he starts causing trouble. It will keep him quiet. He'll be there only three weeks or so. Then he'll go to the adolescent unit at Fulton or Farmington."

"All right, Doctor."

"Thank you, Sister."

I hung up.

Nick Portini walked through the emergency room on his way to the parking lot. He's a urologist.

He stopped and spoke to me. "I saw Paul Farnsworth in the admission office just now and I asked who was sick. He said it was one of his kids and that you're taking care of him. What's the trouble?"

Nick gossips. He's "upwardly mobile," as the current jargon puts it. He married a girl with good social connections and he's going from North End Italian to South Side WASP in one generation.

"He has a nervous kid," I replied.

"Is that all?"

"More or less. We all have our troubles."

Nick patted me on the shoulder and walked on.

I then disposed of Matthew's narcotic kit and heroin supply in the manner I had told him I would, and I looked at my watch. It was almost 12:00. I telephoned my secretary. "Marie, I'm running late. I'll eat lunch here at St. Catharine's and I'll be in the office about a quarter to one."

97

She told me she'd been through the mail, had thrown out all the advertisements and other junk, had filled in the insurance forms, taking the diagnoses from my files, and had left a couple of things on my desk for me. There was one telephone call, from Dr. Frank Thompson.

"It's probably a consultation, Marie. He calls only for that. Call him and explain that I'm tied up at St. Catharine's. Get the basic data on the patient and a general idea of what the problem is. Give him an appointment for the patient. If it's obviously a hospital case—an overdose of pills or a delusional schizophrenic—call me at the coffee shop here at St. Catharine's. Thanks."

Mrs. Goncalvez came over. She's the head nurse in the emergency room on the day shift.

"Dr. Chapman, could you give us diagnoses on these two cases of yours that were in here in December and January? The record office is on our necks to get our back records cleaned up."

I reached out my hand for the two sheets.

Mr. McNamara. December 29. One of the usual run of post-Christmas depressions. He took sixteen sleeping pills and came in comatose. I admitted him through the emergency room, and he recovered.

Mrs. Bartlett. January 11. Another Christmas casualty with much the same history as Mr. McNamara. I filled in the data and put the papers on Mrs. Goncalvez's desk.

Christmas, fortunately, comes but once a year. It stirs up painful emotional turmoil of the past and unites families that would be better off apart. For six weeks afterward psychiatrists' telephones ring off their hooks as family physicians and internists funnel them in to us. I once kept track, and a little less than 25 percent of my year's new cases came in the six weeks after Christmas. Every psychiatric service in town, except hulking old Elmdale Hospital, is full, and I constantly have three or four patients at their homes on sedation waiting for beds. Scrooge was right, before he reformed. Christmas, bah! Humbug!

6

AT a little before 12:00 I entered the coffee shop at St. Catharine's, sat down at a table with Dave Marbeck, and ordered a couple of grilled cheese sandwiches, a salad, and a glass of milk. Joe Turner, Tom Lyman, and Murray Walker sat down with us. Five doctors circling a small round table for lunch.

In novels and on television programs doctors discuss medical research and perplexing cases. Life is a little different.

Dave: I got held up at Lutheran United and didn't get here until ten thirty. I drove through the parking lot three times and didn't find a damn opening. I finally had to park two blocks away on the Pembroke Mall and hoof it over here. God damn! The board of directors are always talking about what they can do to help the doctors. What we need is more parking space. But you just try to tell them that. They know as much about running a hospital as I know about running a spaceship.

Joe: We have a committee on that.

Dave: Committee, hell! We've had ten committees on that. And they never do anything. All they do is study the matter for eight months and then work out a method for

100

repainting the yellow lines in the parking lot so they can squeeze in a couple of more cars.

Tom: Yeah, and they do it by making every slot smaller so we can smash our fenders getting in and out.

Dave: And then there are those delivery trucks. It seems to me that they could make their deliveries before eight in the morning instead of waiting until nine or ten, when all the doctors are trying to get in. There was a Sure-Way Dairy truck last week that smashed into the rear of Herb McKay's car, and they had to call the police to make out a report before the damn truck driver would move his truck. And you couldn't get in from the Oak Street side all morning. There must have been fifteen doctors piled up in Oak Street before someone got out and went in to see what the trouble was, and then he came out, and they all had to go around to the other side. And there was a terrible mess with everybody trying to get in and out of that one-way exit.

Tom: They can't do anything about those delivery trucks. The unions won't let them change the drivers' hours unless they give them special pay or some damn thing. We went into all this last year.

Joe: Then why doesn't the hospital tear down that big old house they bought behind the hospital, clear off the space, and make a larger parking lot for the doctors?

Tom: The nuns are putting the practical-nursing students in there.

Dave: Well, I don't have anything against the sisters, but if you ask me, they're too damn economical. This hospital has enough reserve funds to do something about this problem. Hell! This hospital owns all those old houses and run-down two-story apartment buildings all the way up Thirty-ninth Street.

Tom: They're all rented.

101

Dave: Well, unrent them.

Tom: The sisters don't want to lose the income. They say they need it for modernization or something.

Dave: Well, why don't they modernize the parking lot? They're too damn tight with their money, that's what they are. The least they could is move those practical-nursing students into some other building, tear down the one they're in, and enlarge the doctors' parking lot. When there's a lot of snow, it's a mess.

Tom: They really don't want to do anything until they decide whether or not they're going to merge some of their facilities with Bethesda. Between St. Catharine's and Bethesda they own most of the land between the two hospitals. And if they work out some master plan, they can get government funds and tear down the whole five blocks and rebuild the area at the government's expense.

Dave: That'll take years, decades. I won't live to see it.

I said: The board of directors of Bethesda won't wait that long.

Joe: They'll have to. Anyway, with the number of nuns going down every year and the number of lay administrators going up in St. Catharine's, they'll work it out in another year or two.

Dave: I don't think my car will last that long.

That ended this subject.

Murray: Did you hear what old Meinert's doing?

Dave: What's he been up to?

Murray: He's divorcing his wife and marrying his secretary.

Joe: At his age! He's sixty-five if he's a day.

Murray: Still, he's doing it. My wife knows his wife pretty well and got it straight from her. It seems it's been going on for a long time. His secretary's been with him for ten years. She's a good-looking girl. I've seen her making

102

rounds with him. He puts a white uniform on her and tells the patients she's his nurse. But she's no more a nurse than I'm an Eskimo.

Joe: But he's Catholic, and his patients are mainly from old-time German and Irish Catholic families. This won't do his practice any good. He's a fool. Why doesn't he just go on as he is—keep his wife and his secretary, too?

Murray: His wife pushed him. She caught the two of them together somewhere or other a year ago and told him to get rid of her or she'd divorce him. And he knew what that would do to his practice. So he said he'd get rid of her. But he stalled and he didn't do it. So they went on bluffing and counterbluffing each other, and threatening and counterthreatening, until finally his wife saw a lawyer, and then the fat was in the fire.

Dave: Meinert's fat, that is.

Murray: Yeah, but now it's the other way around. He wants a divorce, but she just wants a legal separation. She says she'll be damned if she's going to turn him lose to marry that little gold digger, and he says he'll do what he damn pleases and get a Mexican or Nevada divorce if it comes to that.

Joe: Good lord! Sixty-five years old, and he's got two women fighting over him. I hope I'm still going that strong when I'm sixty-five.

Murray: Yeah, but I agree that it's not going to do his practice any good.

I said: Well, they can just live happily ever after on his Social Security checks and Medicare.

Silence.

Munching.

Tom: Did you see Lloyd Davis' write-up in the *Star*?

Dave: Yeah, my wife showed it to me.

Tom: The medical society ought to do something about

103

that kind of publicity. It's unethical. There was a whole damn page in the Sunday *Star* about him, and his big-game hunting trips in East Africa, and his wife's painting, and his kid's skiing in Norway, and God only knows what else. And those pictures. Him with his foot on a lion's head. The guide probably shot the thing. In fact, I heard that those governments don't let them shoot lions anymore because they're getting so scarce, and it was probably a stuffed lion. And the title of the article—something about one of Kansas City's leading physicians being "a man for all seasons" or some hackneyed crap like that.

It may be noted in passing that Tom and Lloyd Davis both practice the same specialty in the same office building and cast their nets for patients in the same social circles.

Joe: How does a guy get a write-up like that?

Tom: How does he get it? Because Stan Ackley of the *Star,* who wrote it, is one of his patients. And Lloyd Davis soft-soaps everybody, especially anybody who can do him any good. He tells them all that they're sick as hell and then saves their lives. Bullshit!

Dave: I saw the article. You can't deny that he wrote those two books it mentioned.

Tom: Wrote them, hell! There are ghost-writers in these college towns who for four or five thousand dollars will do library research and write a book on anything from Einstein's theory of relativity to how to screw a baboon. And for another five or six thousand bucks there are a couple of medical publishing companies that will publish them, and you're an author. And you hand out nine hundred copies to nine hundred patients, and the publisher sells fifty and two years later junks the other fifty. It's a racket. My brother-in-law is a big-time orthopedist in Milwaukee, and he does the same thing with the same

104

damn publishing house that puts out Lloyd Davis' books. And it's all tax deductible as a professional expense. So for about ten thousand bucks you're an author, and you make it all back in a bigger practice the first year afterward.

Joe: Don't get excited, Tom. It'll stir up your ulcer again.

Tom: Lloyd Davis could no more write a book than I could run an atom smasher. I've seen some of his consultation notes. He's almost illiterate.

I said: There's a headline for the *Star:* ILLITERATE KANSAS CITY DOCTOR WRITES TWO BOOKS ON HEART DISEASE.

Tom gave me a disgusted look and went on: It's no laughing matter. That sort of crap impressed the hell out of patients and is bad for all of us.

Especially you, I thought, and bit into my second cheese sandwich.

Joe: Well, a lot of fellows do it or something like that.

Tom: Oh, a little bit is all right. You can overlook a guy who puts it in the society column every time his mother-in-law visits him or he goes to Hawaii for ten days. But Lloyd Davis goes too far—a whole damn page in the Sunday Kansas City *Star.*

Dave: Aw, nobody reads that stuff. Who the hell pays any attention to the Kansas City *Star?* The people get their news on television now.

Tom: A lot of people read it. People like to read about doctors. They think we're a bunch of noble crusaders running around saving lives and all that sort of thing.

I said: Well, make a complaint to the medical society if you want to.

Tom: What good would that do? They wouldn't do anything. Don't rock the boat. That's their motto.

Dave: Tom, people are not all that dumb. That kind of

publicity cuts two ways. Who wants a doctor who's hunting lions in Africa when you have your coronary? And on top of that, they're afraid of the bills that such a big shot might send them.

Tom: Still, somebody should do something about it.

Joe: At any rate, Lloyd Davis is peanuts compared to the guys at the med school. They're always on TV, or in the paper, or lecturing some women's club. At least once a month they announce some "great scientific discovery" they've just made.

Dave: They say they have to have good exposure in the media, since most of their funds are voted by the legislature every year. They've got to have a raving public behind them.

Joe: Yeah, but enough is enough. Most of them are duds who couldn't make it in private practice if they tried or weirdos who do research on rats and wouldn't know what to do with a patient if they met one. Most of us are more competent than they are, and you know it. They're afraid to leave the ivory tower.

Tom: Yeah, but with all the publicity the med school gets, they attract people into the private-patient setup over there. They've scooped up a few of my patients lately, especially the well-heeled ones.

Joe: Exactly. Pretty soon it'll get to be fashionable to go over to the med school and be treated by the professors and the little geniuses who assist them. If we don't watch out, in ten years we'll be treating colds and sprained ankles, and all the rest of it will be going into the private-patient section of the med school.

Dave: They ought to stick to their clinic patients and research and leave the private patients alone.

Joe: Look at it this way. They have no overhead and no

staff to pay. They have a state-financed office and hospital under one roof. They're treating private patients in a setup that's subsidized by taxpayers' money. And they give damn poor service at that. They work everybody up for Cushing's disease, and Addison's disease, and half a dozen other rare diseases that you see once every ten years. And then they tell the patient he's in good shape. But the public eats it up.

Tom: On top of that, they're unethical. They talk to the patients about us as if we're a bunch of duffers who don't know anything that's happened in medicine in the last ten years. They talk as if we should have discovered some disease, which the patient probably doesn't have anyway, five years ago. They sell him a bill of goods, and once a patient gets over there they keep referring him around from one specialty to another ad infinitum.

Dave: Yeah, but some of my patients who've gone over there are now trailing back, especially after they get the bills for all those lab tests. Those guys don't have the human touch. They give them a two-week workup, a one-minute summary, and send them home. The public eventually gets tired of that.

Tom: Because it's socialized medicine. They get their salaries regardless of whether the patients are satisfied or not.

Dave: Sure, and who wants a nine-to-five, five-day-a-week doctor?

Tom: Well, maybe so. But all the same, they ought not to go on TV once a month and announce that they've just discovered the cure for some deadly disease.

Dave: Granted.

A moment of silence while medical mastication continued.

Joe: Tom, how's your new office building coming along?

Tom: Fine. We ought to be in it by the middle of May. We're going to have an open house on the Sunday before we start seeing patients there. You'll all get invitations. Come on out and see it. The place is a beaut, if I do say so.

Joe: I'll be there, especially if there are free drinks.

Tom: There will be.

I said: I'll be there. I'd like to see the place; I've heard it's rather fancy.

Dave: How much is the building going to cost you?

Tom: It's running more than we expected.

Joe: It always does. These architects, builders, and interior decorators think doctors are made of money.

Tom: However, it's worth it.

Dave: Yeah, but how much is it going to run?

Tom: Well, about seven hundred and fifty thousand dollars.

Murray: Seven hundred and fifty thousand dollars! That's a hell of a lot of money.

Tom: I know, but it's worth it. And our accountant says it's reasonable.

Murray: Just how does your accountant come to the conclusion that it's reasonable for four internists to spend seven hundred and fifty thousand dollars tearing down a large old suburban house and building a four-man medical clinic?

Tom: A doctor's office is his workshop. He needs the proper space and facilities to do his job.

Murray: That sounds like something your architect told you. Why the hell didn't you just remodel that old house and do it for one-third or one-fourth the money? It was a lovely old house. Judge McKinley lived there years ago. I remember the place.

Tom: We tore it down because we wanted a modern building suited to our needs.

108

Murray: Huh! That sounds like more architect talk to me.

I said: Lay off him, Murray.

I felt uncomfortable, and I think a couple of others did, as Murray began to badger Tom. Murray has a hostile streak in him, and sometimes he nags. He may be worth listening to, but not at lunch.

Murray: All I'm doing is asking the man about his new office.

Tom: Moreover, as our accountant points out, it's a good investment. That property is fairly near the Johnson County Freeway, and it's bound to go up in value. We have a sizable piece of land; we need it for parking space. In twenty years the land alone will probably be worth what we've put into the building. Moreover, many of my patients are moving out there, and they expect a physician to have adequate facilities to deal with their problems.

Murray: You have a smooth-talking accountant or architect or both.

Tom: Damn it, I spend one-fourth of my life in my office, and I'm entitled to a convenient, comfortable place to work in. Moreover, an internist needs space. He needs an electrocardiogram room, a small lab, examination rooms, washrooms, and the rest of it. And with building costs what they are, seven hundred and fifty thousand dollars is reasonable.

Murray: Reasonable, my ass. You and your patients will spend the rest of your lives paying for it.

Joe: Calm down, fellows.

Murray: And if you start to figure out how four middle-aged suburban internists are going to pay off seven hundred and fifty thousand dollars, plus interest, plus this and plus that, over a twenty-year period, it'll end up a third more than that. And you and your partners can't afford that any more than I can afford a trip to the moon.

Tom: I don't see what the hell my office has to do with you.

Murray: And one more thing. Does that seven hundred and fifty thousand dollars include the interior decorating and the medical equipment?

Tom: It includes the medical equipment.

Murray: And the interior decorating?

Tom: Well, no.

Murray: And for that you've probably got some fag who'll make the place look like a high-class antique shop or a room in the Nelson Art Gallery, and there won't be a comfortable chair in the whole place. Those queers always spend three times more than they say they're going to, especially if they can drag the doctors' wives into the act.

Tom: There's nothing wrong with our interior decorator.

Murray: What's his name?

Tom: It's none of your damn business.

Murray: Huh! I'll see him when I go to your open house. He'll be prancing around, showing off his masterpiece.

Tom: I'll make sure you don't get an invitation.

Joe: Now, boys, break it up. That was the bell. Go to your corners and settle down.

Dave: Anyway, Murray, it's no skin off your ass if Tom wants to spend seven hundred and fifty thousand dollars . . .

Murray: Plus decorating expenses.

Dave: . . . on his office. What difference does it make to you?

Murray: It's just that I think he's getting in over his head, that's all. It's bad for him, his partners, and his patients. Between them, they're going to have to sweat to pay for this thing. And the patients know it. I went to the open house of the Brookwood Clinic out in Clifton, and some guy next to

110

me nudged his wife and said, "So this is why you've been coming here for shots once a week for eight months."

Joe: They spent too much at Brookwood.

Murray: And as a result, all nine of them have ended up so strapped for money that they're fighting with each other, and half of them will hardly talk to the other half, but they owe so damn much money that they have to go on working together for the next twenty years. A fancy office doesn't impress the public anymore; it frightens them.

Dave: Let's talk about the Royals and the Chiefs.

Tom: Hell! The public would complain no matter what we did. If we practiced for nickels and dimes in phone booths, they'd say it was too much. Anyway, what the hell do you want me to do—tear down my new office, move into a downtown storefront, and get mugged every night as I get into my car?

Murray: You simply could have remodeled Judge McKinley's old house, asphalted the front yard for a parking lot, and spent one-fourth as much money. And both you and your patients would be better off. Especially you. The average American doctor spends two-thirds of his time working for overhead and taxes, and some are worse than that.

Joe: Yeah, my overhead is forty percent of my gross. My accountant keeps telling me I should cut it down.

Murray: And think of all the things you could do with that money. A few doctors are rich, but the average doctor is not. Why, when Don Patterson died last year his wife had to go back to work as a nurse to make ends meet. She's saving his insurance money to put the kids through college.

Joe: So I suppose I should get a horse and buggy, and a tall black hat, and start making house calls.

Dave: If the energy crisis gets worse, it may come to that.

111

Laughter broke the tension a little.

Joe: Anyway, it's hospital costs the public bitches most about, and the way their insurance premiums keep bouncing up to cover them.

Murray: There's a lot that could be done about that.

Tom: Are you running for Congress or something?

Joe: He'd never be elected.

Murray: Listen, look at that new wing they put up at Lutheran United. Colored television in every room, beds that go up and down by electric buttons, two-way communication between every bed and the nursing station, three computers—and nobody knows what the hell to do with two of them—and every room is outfitted with wires and tubes for electrocardiograms, suction, and Lord knows what else. Why, the employees' dining room alone is fancier than half the restaurants in Kansas City. And who needs all that marble and oak paneling in the lobby, the director's office, and the board room? And those corridors —you could drive a delivery truck down them.

Dave: Yeah, some of the patients call it the Lutheran United Hilton Hotel.

Murray: They could have done it all for half the money. But the board of directors are all fat-cat businessmen who haven't the faintest idea how the average man lives. Hospital boards and half the doctors have no conception what a fifty-dollar bill looks like to the man in the street.

Dave: Well, interesting as all this crap has been, I must now go to my overly expensive office and save a few lives.

Joe: Yeah, and next time you come to lunch, Murray, leave your soapbox at home.

Tom: Next time? There's not going to be any next time. This is the last time I have lunch with Comrade Murray Walker.

Dave: Aw, come on, fellows, bury the hatchet.

112

Tom: Only in his skull.

Murray: Tom, when I have my coronary, I'll call you. How's that?

Tom: Great! I'll look forward to it.

A few laughs smoothed out some of the wrinkles.

We all got up, paid our checks, and left.

At 12:45 I arrived in my office. The waiting room was empty except for a pharmaceutical-firm salesman. I nodded at him and went into my office.

Marie came in and I gave her a few bits of data for a couple of insurance forms. I quickly ran through the two pieces of mail on my desk.

"Send in the salesman," I said to Marie as she left.

He came in. Pharmaceutical salesmen (or "detail men," as they often are called, since their main job is to give physicians the details on new drugs produced by their firms) all present pretty much the same façade to physicians. They have similar black or brown satchels, the same kind of quick, earnest chatter, and the same agreeable smiles. I give each of them two minutes, and they know my system. They have to "make contact" with every doctor in their district at least once every sixty to ninety days; they must make their pitches and leave their samples. They can't have too many blank spaces on their monthly reports. Live and let live.

The salesman came in, shook hands, opened his satchel, and started.

"Doctor, I think we have a new product that will interest you. Anxiety and depression are two of the commonest problems that you and all other physicians see in your practice. For years many firms have been looking for one medication that will handle both of these problems. Our firm has just launched Ambitrax. It's a combination of a minor tranquilizer for anxiety and an antidepressant for depression. You can see from this reading material that I'll leave with you that—"

"Okay," I said, "what other miracle drugs are you launching this month?"

He laughed. "Doctor, we have studies from a University of California group—"

"I know," I said. "Twenty-five years ago I did one of those studies. The man from the drug company and I got pretty friendly, and he told me that a pharmaceutical company usually could tell what a research team's report would be before they got it. Some investigators are bubbling enthusiasts and feel that all drugs help, and others are pessimists who send them negative results. How do you measure fluctuating anxiety and depression in a psychoneurotic? If you load your questions right, you can get whatever results you want and interpret them any way that suits you."

He laughed and shook his head in pleasant disagreement. That's his job. Most pharmaceutical representatives laugh and shake their heads at me in much the same manner. They are trained how to handle all kinds of retorts and questions.

"Well, give it a try, Doctor," he said as he piled samples of this wonder drug on my desk.

"Do you have any samples of Tribrium?" I asked. Marie takes it when she can't sleep.

He pulled a couple of small bottles of it from the bottom of his bag.

"And any barbiturate?"

"Not with me. But I'll be back in this building again at the end of the week and leave a couple of bottles of Marbate, our barbiturate for both daytime and nightime sedation." He made a note in his pocket notebook.

114

"Frankly," I said, "the barbiturates are as good as all the rest of the sedatives and tranquilizers except the phenothiazines, and they cost one-tenth as much since the patents on them have run out."

"But the public doesn't like barbiturates, Doctor," he replied. "They have a bad name with the average man in the street."

"I know," I said. "The people want Science, and barbiturates are not Science."

"I suppose you don't need any more calendars by this time of year?" he inquired.

"All my maiden aunts have papered their walls with them," I answered.

He laughed again, thanked me for my time, and left.

7

1:00. My first patient of the afternoon was Pattie Whitman. I went to the door and saw her in the waiting room. I nodded to her and she came in.

I waited for her to begin.

She commented on the weather and I agreed that it was a nasty day.

She began. "Nothing much has happened. Everything has gone on about as usual, except that we've been unusually busy at the store for this time of year. My father has been pretty tense because my stepmother has been giving him a hard time. She wakes up at night and thinks she's dying. So she wakes him up, and one night last week she insisted that he take her to Mt. Sinai, and so he did, and the doctor in the emergency room said it was just nerves—anxiety. She's upset about her daughter Gloria. Things are not going too well between her and her husband. They may break up, and they've only been married for two years."

And so Pattie went on talking at random about the things that were going on at the store, on her dates, in her apartment (she lived separately from her father and stepmother), and in other areas of her life. I asked questions occasionally, made some comments, and gave her advice on a few minor points.

116

Pattie was a good-looking, single, thirty-five-year-old woman who came to see me once a week, every Monday at 1:00, and had done so for almost fourteen years. No one except us knew that she came; it was our secret. She paid me in cash and told her father and the personnel at their store that she routinely took a long lunch break on Mondays to do some shopping. She virtually ran her father's large jewelry store in midtown Kansas City. He was in his late seventies. Pattie's brother was a gambler who chased girls; he came to the store once a week to get money from Pattie.

Our sessions are little more than conversations, friendly chitchat, professionally dispensed. I am not entirely sure why Pattie comes to see me, but perhaps it is because I am the only one who knows everything about her and the one person whom she more or less trusts.

Pattie's father had come to America from Poland in the 1920's, a penniless immigrant in his late teens. A cousin in Kansas City gave him a job in his store, and after he learned enough English, he became the bookkeeper and cashier. After he had been in Kansas City several years, he met Pattie's mother. She had a shriveled arm, the residual of a badly set fracture in her childhood. Because of her deformed arm and her plain, pimpled face, she was considered so poor a marriage candidate that her father, though not well-to-do, put a fifteen-thousand-dollar dowry on her and turned her over to a marriage broker. He mated her with Pattie's father and guided the two of them to the marriage canopy. With the fifteen thousand dollars Pattie's father opened a jewelry store. By selling on credit at high interest rates, fencing stolen goods at the back entrance, staying open fourteen hours a day six days a week, and tearing up invoices to avoid taxes, he prospered. In twenty years he was well-to-do, and a decade later he was rich.

The marriage was a horror. Pattie's father, a wiry man

under five feet tall, was a screaming bully. He yelled at his wife and sometimes hit her, and she fought back, shrieking and slapping at him. They worked side by side in the store, wheedling with customers in English and wrangling behind the counter in Yiddish. Their life consisted of the store and their home, which was ten minutes away by bus. Into this cockpit Pattie and her brother Harold were born.

Harold was born first, and like many firstborn Jewish boys of an older generation, he was pampered and spoiled; he grew from a temper-tantrumish brat into a self-centered, demanding adolescent. When such firstborn boys have talent, they may become successful but arrogant business or professional men. Harold had little ability, and he developed into an immature, screaming man who gambled, philandered, and lived off his father. He married a passive girl whom he browbeat, and they were rearing three children, two of whom already had severe phobias.

Pattie was born nine years after her brother, and her parents had no more children. She was a girl, and she came at a time when she was not wanted. After her birth her parents' marital troubles grew worse, and what had been a miserable marriage became a nightmare. However, the Jews of past generations neither divorced nor became alcoholics. They simply suffered and ground on.

When I was a small boy, I asked my mother why the Hertzmans who lived down the street were Jews. She said that the Jews had a somewhat different religion, that they were good, hard-working people, and that they had fine, close family lives. My mother was wrong about their family lives. A psychiatrist soon learns that behind the façades of united harmony in many Jewish families lurk competitiveness, hatreds, envy, and agony. The older Jews reared more than their share of emotionally upset children, and to this day most psychiatrists see far more Jewish patients than would be expected from their percentage of the general

118

population. The modern Jews are much more flexible; they divorce, drink, take drugs, gamble, and philander (both men and women) as much as their non-Jewish neighbors. Whether or not later generations of psychiatrists will see fewer Jewish patients remains to be seen.

Pattie's father dominated the people around him—at the store, at home, and elsewhere—by playing them off against each other, and Pattie became a brickbat in his constant battles with his wife. When Pattie was nasty to her mother, he petted her, told her that her mother was an intolerable woman, and that he was the only one who loved Pattie. After particularly hideous scenes at home he gave her money to go to the movies, to get away from that "hellhole." When his wife ranted at Pattie and drove her from the room, he sided with his wife and told her that Pattie had a touch of Samael and other devils in her. Pattie eavesdropped and heard him playing these dirty games. By keeping them continually at each other's throats, he controlled them both.

Pattie was bright and pretty, but this only heightened her deformed mother's fury against her, and it gave her father more opportunities for pitting his family members against one another. He taunted Pattie's brother with her intelligence, her high marks at school, and her acumen at the store. He made Pattie and Harold enemies; he indulged Harold's every whim, but was niggardly with Pattie and flailed her with guilt-laden harangues.

However, at the store he made use of Pattie's brightness. She began to spend time at the store when she was five, and by the time she was eight she was working there. Telephone books were piled on a stool and she ran the cash register for several hours at a time. Her father trusted none of his employees, and only members of the family were allowed to touch the cash register.

By the time she was ten Pattie knew clearly that neither

parent loved her, that her brother hated her, and that her father exploited her cruelly at home and at the store. She felt guilty about the anger within her, and at times she was flooded by an eerie dread that verged on panic and had no name.

Each weekday she went to school from eight to three and waited on customers or ran the cash register in the store from three to seven. Then she went home, ate dinner alone, studied, and went to bed. On Saturdays she worked in the store from seven in the morning until nine at night. On Sundays she hid from her mother in the morning and went to the movies in the afternoon and at night.

It was only at school that she found companionship that did not hurt her. Although her parents were well-to-do, they lived in a working-class neighborhood in a large, musty, unkempt old house with a weedy garden behind. At school she was the only Jewish girl in her class. Her father had changed his name from Weissman to Whitman when he came to America, and few of her classmates knew she was Jewish. However, it would have made little difference; to working-class girls and boys of that time Jews were people they read about in the Bible but rarely met.

By the time Pattie reached middle childhood she had become the secretive, cautious, untrusting girl she was to be for the rest of her life. Reared in a home where she experienced only fury, rejection, and exploitation, she expected no more from the world. Relationships with people were traps; once they got you they tormented you. It was best not to get close to anyone. Still, the kids around her at school seemed strangely lighthearted and free. Maybe there was something more in life than learning not to be hurt; however, it would be too dangerous to find out.

Pattie was always at the top of her class and skipped a year in grade school. She had a pretty smile that she used constantly to defend herself; from behind it she peered at the world with frightened eyes. When she entered adolescence, the boys began to pay attention to her—freckle-faced boys with broad grins, carefree ways, and jalopy cars. But a good Jewish girl didn't date *goyish* boys; this had been hammered into her. Though she chatted with boys in high school corridors, she turned them down on dates, and in time they gave up and went away.

When Pattie was sixteen, her mother began to have abdominal pain; she vomited and grew thin. She went to the hospital, where she had X-ray studies and many tests, and the doctors found that she had cancer of the stomach. They operated, but could not remove it all; she had much X-ray treatment, and then she came home to die. The hospital frightened Pattie's mother, and she would not stay there.

She spent four months dying during a hot Missouri summer. Her mother could not stand the windows of her room to be closed, and so there was no air conditioning; day and night electric fans blew the heat, and her mother's room stank of vomit, sweat, and half-dead flowers. Pattie was her nurse; other relatives and practical nurses tried to attend her, but she clung to Pattie. Half clouded by morphine to dull her increasing pain, she alternately shrieked curses at Pattie and begged her forgiveness. She talked of long-dead relatives and spoke fearfully of the fire of Gehenna. One minute she showered Pattie with caresses and sobbed that she had never loved her as she ought and the next moment she screamed that Pattie's torment had caused her cancer. By the time her mother died Pattie had lost thirty pounds and she shambled about as if she were in a trance.

The funeral was on a hot September morning. That afternoon her father went to the store and her brother played poker. Pattie went home and wandered alone about the house. She was sitting on the edge of her bed when abruptly she felt that someone was watching her. She looked at the door and saw her mother, pale and emaciated, glaring at her. Pattie screamed and ran from the house. She got into her car and raced out onto the lonely dirt and asphalt roads in the countryside. Speed gave her some relief. Suddenly Pattie looked to one side. Her mother was staring in the car window and was yelling at her. Then her mother was on the hood of the car.

Pattie did not go to school that year. For three months she wandered about the countryside in her car each morning and went to the movies every afternoon and evening. Sometimes she saw the same movie three or four times. Her father's cajolings, her relatives' reproaches, and her brother's taunts had no effect on her. Then, as Christmas came, she saw and heard her mother less. One day, a week before Christmas, Pattie went to the store and took up her old place silently behind the cash register. Her father came up and patted her on the shoulder; he said she was a good girl and gave her fifty dollars "to buy something nice for yourself."

For the rest of that school year Pattie worked in the store from seven in the morning until closing time and had lunch brought in from a neighboring café. She became a shrewder merchant than her father and the best salesperson in the store. She had a way with customers. She smiled, fondled the merchandise, fastened the wristwatch or broach on the customer's wrist or blouse, and she didn't stop her gentle stream of talk until the sale was made. She dealt with the dapper thieves who came to the back of the store to sell stolen watches and rings, and she spent Sundays falsifying books and inventory lists to reduce taxes. Always smiling, she watched her father's employees sharply and caught them carrying out the trinkets and watchbands with which

122

they increased their small salaries. Her father praised her and perhaps became a little afraid of her. He no longer could bully her. If he criticized her, she stared silently at him, and he went away. She had no friends.

When September came, she went back to high school and completed her last year. In March of that year a representative of a small but well-known liberal arts college in Minnesota came to her high school. The college was seeking bright students from other states to broaden the geographical area from which it drew its student body. The college representative interviewed Pattie and offered her a small scholarship, though she did not need it. She told her father, and being caught unprepared, he wasn't sure what to say. "Take it," he said, and she did.

Afterward he regretted his words and offered Pattie a new car and one thousand dollars in cash if she would go to a junior college in Kansas City and work evenings and weekends in the store. He offered her a handsome weekly salary, complained that he was getting old, said that she was his right hand in the business, cursed her brother as a worthless bum, and begged her to stay with him. But each time he pleaded and cried she said, "Then why did you tell me to take it?" In time he gave up, and that fall Pattie went away to college.

At college she lived in a dormitory with sixty chattering, lively girls, and she began to date the flaxen-headed boys who lived in other dormitories. Her girlfriends invited her home for holidays, and during the summers she worked in a camp in Canada that was run by the family of one of her classmates. She went home only occasionally, fleeing her father's complaints and pleas that she spend her vacations working with him. However, her father never skimped on the money he sent her, nor did he ever use threats of stopping it as a tool to get her to come home.

During her third year at college Pattie's father remarried.

He married an attractive widow twenty years younger than himself, and she brought two insolent adolescent children with her. She was an immature, silly, frightened woman who continually went to doctors for emotionally caused symptoms. However, it pleased Pattie's father to have a good-looking wife twenty years younger than himself, and she was a stupid woman whom he could easily outmaneuver and dominate.

When Pattie came home for the spring vacation to meet her new stepmother, she found the house (now a better one in a fashionable neighborhood) taken over by the stepmother and her children. Her stepmother regarded her as an intruder and was peevish and nasty toward her. Her father told Pattie that her stepmother was "all right but a little nervous." However, cunning, cautious Pattie saw it as it was and went back to college after three days.

Four months before her graduation from college Pattie's father had a severe heart attack, and Pattie at once came home from college to see him. She found her father half conscious in the hospital and her stepmother a frightened, agitated woman who now treated Pattie in a quite different way. If her father died, all his property and the store would go to Pattie and her brother. The stepmother would receive nothing, since they had married in the old-fashioned Jewish way, with a civil contract as well as a religious ceremony. The contract stipulated that in the event of the death of either of them, his children would receive what he brought into the marriage and acquired for himself thereafter, and the spouse would receive nothing. The stepmother had little property, and she received Pattie with caresses and fear.

When Pattie arrived at the hospital, her father groggily demanded to be taken out of his oxygen tent for a few minutes to talk to her. He reached out a feeble hand and

124

grasped hers. "When I get well," he mumbled, "I won't be able to work as I always have. You must come back to the store. Only you can run it. Your brother is no good. Without you they'll steal everything, take care of nothing, and smash the store in a year. Your mother and I worked for nickels and dimes in that store for twenty-five years. I need you. If you don't come back, I'll work myself to death in a year, and it will be your fault. Come back. Give me your promise that you'll come back."

Pattie sobbed and gave her promise. Five days later she went back to college. Her father did not die. In six weeks he was at home, sleeping in a bed on the first floor. In another eight weeks he was spending three hours a day at the store. Each week he wrote Pattie a letter full of complaints and reminded her of her promise. Her stepmother called her once a week to tell her how bad her father was and told her she must come home or he would kill himself working in the store. She said she would introduce Pattie to lots of fine Jewish boys, and she could have her pick of them.

Before her father became sick, Pattie had been accepted for graduate work in a major university on the West Coast, and two of her college classmates had planned to room with her there.

The horrid past reached out to gather Pattie in, and the four good years she had had at college were slipping away. A weird agony filled her. One night three weeks before graduation she looked up from her books and saw her mother standing in a corner of the room. Her mother did not leave her after that. She yelled in Pattie's ears, looked in at her from windows, flitted ahead of her in corridors, and roamed wildly through her dreams. Soon her dreams and waking hours blended into one eerie mass of terror.

Her brother and an uncle went to the college and brought her home. The college excused her from her final examinations and awarded her her degree. She spent six months on the psychiatric ward at Mt. Sinai under my care. Twice she appeared to recover, but she relapsed when she faced leaving the hospital. Then I cut out all visits from relatives for three months, kept her on moderate doses of an antipsychotic medication, organized a good activities program for her, and spent three hours a week talking with her. She got well and stayed well.

Pattie is now a woman of thirty-five. Her father is still alive; he spends six hours a day at the store, but leaves its management to her. She also takes care of her father's real estate, his stocks, and other business interests. She gives liberal amounts of money in cash each week to her stepmother and her brother. They know they are in her hands and they are somewhat afraid of her. They give her no trouble, and she gives them none. Her father has changed his will, leaving control of the store and two-thirds of his property to Pattie, after extracting from her a promise that she would see that her stepmother and brother were always well taken care of.

She lives in a large, well-decorated apartment in a fashionable area, alone. She buys an expensive new car each year. She takes a five-day weekend out of town now and then, but has not had a long vacation since she returned to the store three months after she left the hospital. During her twenties a lot of ambitious Jewish boys tried to date her, but she pushed them all away. She now dates only non-Jewish men; she has had a few friendly affairs with them, but she gets close to no one. She dresses well and men turn to look at her on the street.

She has never been sick again. Yet she still comes to see me once a week for fifty minutes of light chitchat. I have learned a lot about the jewelry business. Why does she come to see me? Several times I have suggested that it is not

126

necessary for her to come, but when I do so she gets visibly tense and says that she wants "to keep this link." Is it because I am the only one who really knows her? Is it a superstitious clinging to the person who pulled her out of a horror into which she had fallen and a fear that it might come back again if she broke contact with me? Does she keep me on retainer for any future trouble that might come up, as some people hire tax accountants and lawyers? Or do I represent something far different and more significant in Pattie's life? I don't ask these questions. I've been in this kind of work long enough to know that sometimes it's best to let well enough alone.

It's 1:50. She knows the routine. She glances at her watch. She rises and puts out a white-gloved hand (she has certain old-fashioned habits, such as always wearing white gloves when she goes to the doctor). We shake hands. She gives me the same charming smile she gives everyone.

"Next Monday at one?"

"Certainly."

She leaves. But when she leaves she opens the door and goes out without turning her back to me. She has an intricate, graceful way of doing it. She is the only patient I have who does not turn his back to me as he leaves.

I don't know why she does it.

Marie enters. There are two telephone calls. One is to a pharmacist to renew a prescription, and the other is to a doctor to tell him it's all right to reduce the medication on a patient whom I treated and referred back to him for checkup visits after he recovered.

8

2:00. The next patient is new, a Mrs. Demarest from Millbank, a suburb of Kansas City. She was referred by Dr. Willis Dexter, a family physician. Willis Dexter's referrals are usually good ones. Thirty years ago Willis Dexter was the only doctor in Millbank, and Millbank was a rural village with a population of eight hundred. Today forty thousand people live in Millbank, and Willis Dexter is the senior man in the twelve-doctor Millbank Clinic. Millbank's population is composed mainly of young couples with two or three children, white-collar and blue-collar families. Willis and his busy colleagues do not give a psychoneurotic patient shots and pills for three years until he is perhaps untreatable before they send him to a psychiatrist. If he has a psychiatric problem, they send him to a psychiatrist. Many of my most gratifying cases come from the Millbank Clinic.

I put a couple of eight- by eleven-inch white sheets of notepaper into a clipboard, write Mrs. Demarest's name, address, telephone number, husband's first name, and referring physician's name at the top and date it. I make systematic notes during the first two interviews with most new patients. A busy psychiatrist simply cannot keep all his patients straight if he doesn't. After the first couple of interviews I make four- or five-line summaries after each session.

128

I go to the door. A neatly dressed woman in her late twenties is sitting in the waiting room. I step out, introduce myself, and invite her into my office. She sits down and I shut the door. I suggest that she may begin anywhere that is comfortable or convenient in telling me what kind of problem or anxiousness or symptom brings her to see me. This is merely a broad invitation to talk.

She says she is very tense, that the children get on her nerves, and that she feels like crying at times. However, she doesn't look depressed. She looks scared. She stops talking and crumples a handkerchief.

Silence. I make another attempt to get her to talk; she runs on for another three or four sentences and stalls again.

Between 80 and 90 percent of the patients seen in psychiatric work can carry on useful interviews only if the psychiatrist assumes a fairly active role—making comments, asking questions, and exploring. (In sophisticated groups the number of patients who can carry out meaningful interviews without such help is greater, but such persons constitute a very small percentage of the general population.)

I say, "Well, let's get a little background data," and I begin to ask questions.

She's twenty-eight years old and her husband is thirty. He works as a data processor in an insurance company. They have two children, aged three and five, a three-bedroom house, and no debts except on the house. Do they get along well in the marriage? Yes. Her husband is wonderful to her. Is it really all that good? She laughs slightly. Yes, they really get along well.

I ask about her husband's parents. They live in Kansas City. His father works for the Kansas City Power and Light Company, and his mother does not work outside the home. He has two sisters. One is married and lives in Dallas, and the other attends college in Columbia, Missouri. She says she gets along well with all her in-laws. I ask if she ever has any trouble with her husband's mother. No. She's like another mother to her. I say that she's lucky to have such a good mother-in-law. The talk is flowing smoothly, but I don't know where we're going.

I ask about her parents. They live in Millbank. They moved out there three years ago when their neighborhood in Southeast Kansas City went black. Does she have any brothers or sisters? One, an older brother who lives in Los Angeles; he's married and they see little of him now. I inquire about her mother. Her mother is nervous; she says nothing more about her. I note that and will return to it in a couple of minutes. How does she get along with her father? She's close to him. He's a retired railroad employee. He often comes over to her house during the day and watches the children while she does housework or goes shopping.

We return to her mother. In what ways is her mother nervous? The patient stalls. Then she says that her mother has headaches. I ask if she's a fearful woman. No. Domineering? Maybe; she guesses that maybe she is. Does her mother dominate her father? Yes, she always has. Does she scream a lot? Well, yes, when she's mad or upset about something. How often is that? Well, fairly often. Is it especially when she can't have her way? Mrs. Demarest gives a nervous laugh and says yes. We are now picking our way along and learning something about the world of people in which the patient lives and was reared. It is not yet clear whether these data are related to whatever the patient's problem is.

And did her mother scream at her a lot when she was growing up? Not too much. Did she ever talk back to her mother or rebel? No. Never. Well, only when she married. Her mother did not approve of her husband, but she never approved of any of her boyfriends. However, her father took her aside and told her to do what she thought best, but not to tell her mother that he said that. So she eloped, and her mother didn't talk to her for five months. Then they made up. Her mother accepts her husband now, but doesn't really like him.

I ask the patient if she thinks that maybe her mother doesn't like her husband because she can't dominate him. Again she laughs nervously and says yes, perhaps that's it. Her mother and her husband have run-ins every now and then, she adds. I inquire if these quarrels occur mainly when he won't let her mother tell them what to do about something. Yes. I ask if he's the one who really sticks up for the two of them. She guesses that maybe that's it. Is it because she can't stick up for herself to her mother and therefore he does it? That's about it. Has all this changed in any way lately? No. I ask if she feels that these things are in any way related to what brings her to see me. She says no, not really.

I'm beginning to get some concept of the patient, though I still don't know where we're heading.

I inquire if she can get angry and stick up for herself with people when it's necessary. She replies that she doesn't like to argue with people. She feels that it's better to get along with everyone. Does she feel guilty and upset if she gets angry? Yes. Does she feel guilty and upset if somebody gets mad at her? Yes, she feels that people shouldn't fight and argue with each other. Does she feel somewhat upset if she is present when two other people are angry with each other even if she's not involved? Yes, that bothers her, too.

I am silent for a minute or so, to give her an opportunity to pick up the thread and go on, but she cannot. I therefore begin to ask questions again, following the same theme. Can she return defective merchandise to stores and demand her money back? No, her husband is better at that than she is, and so he does it when it needs to be done. Is she like her father in all these respects? Yes, they both are easygoing people who don't see any point in bickering about things.

I inquire if that is one of the reasons why her brother is on the West Coast. Did he go out there to get away from her mother? Maybe, she replies. He and her mother fought all the time. He joined the Marines immediately after he graduated from high school, married in California, and stayed out there after he got out of the Marines. He works for an automobile agency; he does pretty well as a salesman. However, he drinks too much and has been married three times.

I begin to get a feeling about the patient. This girl is afraid of something, and she's so afraid of it that she can't put it into words. An experienced therapist develops intuitions about patients. Intuition is a word used to describe a clinical impression or feeling about a patient that cannot be more clearly defined at the moment. An intuition may be correct or incorrect, but it usually is worth investigating.

I pause. I glance over my two pages of notes.

I ask her if she is afraid of something. She does not answer, but leans forward slightly and squeezes both chair arms. I ask her what she is afraid of. She opens her mouth to say something, but cannot put it into words. I start probing. Is she afraid of illness? She quickly shakes her head from side to side. Is she afraid of death—her own death or that of her husband? No. Is she afraid of mental illness, of losing her mind? She looks hard at me and says nothing. I state slowly and emphatically that apparently she *is* afraid of losing her mind. She shakes her head slightly up and down.

To clear the way for further probing, I give her a broad reassurance. I tell her that from what I've seen and heard so far, I think she has no more chance of losing her mind—that is, of going berserk, running amok, becoming psychotic—than anyone else on the street does. She looks at me doubtfully. I say that with the data I now have, I can give her a 90 percent reassurance that she has little chance of losing her mind, and when I've seen her three or four more times, I shall probably be able to raise that figure to 99 percent. However, this is not the main point I'm driving at, since I now have a fairly good idea where we are heading.

I ask if she sometimes daydreams in a fearful way about things she might do if she became insane. Yes, sometimes, she says. She is staring at me, badly frightened. Does she imagine in dreadful ways that she might do something violent? She runs her tongue slightly over her lips and sits motionless; she dreads where my questions are leading.

Is she afraid, I ask quietly, that she might do something violent to herself? Partly, she responds. To others? Partly, she repeats. To the children, especially? Yes. Does she fear, I ask, that she will murder her children? Yes.

We have finally identified the main symptom that brings her to see me, an obsessive, ruminating dread that she will slaughter her children and that she must be insane or on the verge of becoming so to have such an unnatural thought running through her head day and night. Patients with this kind of obsessive thought usually have such horror of it that they feel that merely putting it into words will break the fragile bonds that hold them back from the terrible acts they feel they are about to perform.

I sit back and with careful emphasis tell her that in my kind of work I frequently see passive young mothers who have fears that they will harm their children. I see about three or four new such cases each year. I indicate, moreover, that they follow a pattern. I ask her, for example, if her dread of harming the children is so great that she is afraid to pick up paring knives and butcher knives in the

133

kitchen, for fear that once the fatal instrument is in her hand she will irresistibly be swept into the bloody act? Yes. Is she, in addition, afraid to be left alone with the children for fear that no one will be there to restrain her once the horrid urge sweeps over her? Yes, yes, that's it. Does she therefore, whenever possible, try to have someone else with her in the house besides the children? Yes.

I then ask her if it seems as if I am reading her mind? With a tense laugh, she says yes. I state that of course, I am not, but that I have seen so many young mothers with fears of this particular kind that I've heard her story many times. Hence, I know the details fairly well. Thus, I can outline some aspects of her fears to her before she tells me about them, and I add that my ability to do so may give her increased confidence in the validity of the reassurances I shall later give her. I state that I have treated many young mothers with such psychoneurotic fears of murdering their children and that none of them has ever done so.

(Mentally ill mothers who on rare occasions murder their children are either hallucinating schizophrenics or delusionally depressed women, and they present far different clinical pictures from mothers with obsessive psychoneurotic fears of infanticide. However, I do not go into these technical matters with Mrs. Demarest, since they would only confuse and upset her and are not relevant to her problems.)

I proceed to point out to her that mothers with her type of problem have no *urge* to harm their children, but rather an obsessive *dread* that they will do so. They are similar to a patient who has an obsessive fear that he will have a heart attack; he does not want to have a heart attack, but cannot rid his mind of the ever-present fear that he is going to have one.

I indicate that such mothers often have characteristic

134

types of fearful daydreams. They envision their pictures on the front pages of the newspapers or on the television screen, showing them as the police lead them away from their homes, disheveled and staring wildly, after they have done the awful deed. They imagine the headlines: MILLBANK MOTHER BUTCHERS CHILDREN. She admits that she has lately had such painful daydreams. I give her strong reassurances that this will never happen, and we go on.

How long has she had these painful fears? Three months. Are they present most of the time, like catchy television advertisement jingles that one cannot get out of his mind? Yes, that's it. And does she feel that anybody who has such weird ideas and "cannot control his thoughts" must be insane or about to become so? Yes, she's felt that way constantly for three months now. I again reassure her that obsessive ideas rarely are the precursors of any kind of psychotic process—that is, going insane or "losing control."

I ask her if she has told her husband about these fears. She says that after she had them a week she told him. What did he say? He told her not to worry about such things and that she wouldn't do it and to forget about it. Wasn't he worried at all? No, he said he was sorry that she was upset about such things, but that she wouldn't do it because she wasn't the type. Has she told anyone else? No. Was she afraid that if she told other people that she had such thoughts they would think she was insane or on the verge of becoming so? Yes. So she had carried this fearful burden almost alone for three months? Yes. She sat back in her chair, let go of the chair arms, and let her hands lie limply in her lap.

I asked her if she had told Dr. Willis Dexter about her fears. No. She tried to, but she broke down crying and couldn't do it. She blurted out that she was very afraid of something but couldn't tell him what it was. And what did Dr. Dexter do? He gave her some tranquilizers and made this appointment to see me.

I then said I was going to give her a brief idea of the kinds of things that may cause her kind of problem. Such explanations in themselves would not solve it, but knowing that it had some rational basis would probably take some of the terror out of it. I added that in a series of systematic interviews, that is, psychotherapy, she had a good chance of getting rid of her fears altogether.

I explained that fearful worries of killing one's children, often coupled with the conviction that one must be insane to think such things, occur most often in very passive young mothers who keep all their anger stored up within themselves and give it no expression in words or acts. After many years of bottling it up, it comes out as this kind of symptom, that is, fearful worries of harming others. In other mothers who never blow off steam, their inner turmoil may come out as stomachaches, or anxiety spells, or other kinds of fears, such as of automobiles or leaving the house.

I indicated that one of the main objects in treating such a mother usually was to help her become aware of the pent-up anger within her and to express at least a part of it occasionally without feeling anxious or guilty about it. Much of this anger had been built up in long-past relationships in her life, although the process of tamping down all assertiveness and aggressiveness was still going on each day. However, expressing angry feelings was not really the most important thing; being aware of them and comfortable with them was more important than any kind of expression that one gave them. This covered the whole range of assertiveness—from being firmer with her bullying mother to being at ease in returning defective merchandise to a store and demanding her money back.

136

I emphasized again that these painful worries were not inexplicable things that descended onto her out of the blue. They had logical causes that we could find as we explored her past and current life situations. For example, I thought we already had discovered some things about her childhood experiences that had molded her into a timid person who felt apprehensive and guilty about any hostile feelings that arose in her.

This, I repeated, was merely a broad outline to help her see that her problem made sense and that we had a lot of work to do in future sessions filling in the details and exploring avenues we had not even approached this time.

Our session was nearly over. I asked her if she had any questions. She said she felt a little better; she asked how often she should come to see me and how long it would last. I said that we should start out at the rate of two sessions a week and then go to once a week, and that treatment, though quite variable in length, usually lasted three to six months. I added that most women with this kind of trouble felt somewhat better after a few interviews.

She asked me about the tranquilizer tablets that Dr. Dexter had prescribed, and I said that they were not too important; she could take them if they helped her. Such a medication sometimes took a small edge off her anxiousness, but the main treatment rested on the psychotherapy. She then asked how much the treatment cost. I told her and said that she could budget it out over a longer period if that was more convenient; she could arrange that with Marie, my secretary, as she was leaving or later.

The interview was over. She smiled, rose, and went to the door. As an afterthought, she turned and asked me if I wanted to speak to her husband. Only if he wanted to see me, I replied. She left.

I picked up the mouthpiece of my dictating machine and dictated a brief courtesy report to Dr. Dexter, which Marie would type later: "Dear Will: I today interviewed your patient Mrs. Emily (Walter) Demarest. This twenty-eight-year-old married woman has a three-month history of the coupled obsessive fears of harming her children and of becoming insane. She has the kind of personality structure that often accompanies this type of obsessive neurotic problem. She is a passive, subnormally assertive person whose childhood experiences have led her to feel anxious and guilty about any expression of aggressive or angry feelings. Her prognosis for improvement during three to six months of psychotherapy is good. I indicated she could continue to take the small doses of tranquilizer that you prescribed if she felt it was useful, but left it up to her. I think she was a little relieved by my initial explanations. Thank you for referring this interesting patient to me. Best wishes, Harry."

Between 1953 and 1957 I treated twenty young mothers with Mrs. Demarest's syndrome of coupled obsessive fears of infanticide and insanity, and one evening I drove over to the medical school library and went through the *Index Medicus* to find something to read on this condition. To my surprise, I found that nothing had ever been written on this fairly common clinical problem. I asked one of the medical librarians to search the literature, and she also found nothing on it. So I gathered my twenty patients' charts together, studied them carefully, and wrote a paper on this type of patient; in the slow course of time and medical publishing, it appeared in a psychiatric journal (*Archives of General Psychiatry,* Vol. 1, July, 1959). In the years since then it gradually has carved itself an apparently secure little niche in the psychiatric literature on obsessive neuroses.

Beginning in 1948, I have written about one such paper each year; there are thirty of them now. This is known as "clinical research"; it consists of reporting the characteris-

138

tics, causes, and treatment of medical disorders. Clinical research contributes to the slow accumulation of medical knowledge, and it provides a background of written experience for later investigators who are attacking a problem and want to review the observations and conclusions of their predecessors. Clinical research also may have some educational value.

Clinical research is contrasted with "investigative research," in which the researcher sets out systematically to examine a problem or to test a hypothesis or a treatment method. I spent six months of my second year of psychiatric residency working under an investigator whom we shall call Dr. Allen. Our chief was keen on research. "We have theories enough in psychiatry," he said. "What we need is not more theories, but more facts."

Dr. Allen was on the trail of facts, or so it was generally believed. He was a bespectacled, lean-faced, earnest man in his middle thirties. He also was on the trail that led to becoming a professor and departmental chairman in a medical school. Like many before him and many after him, he had discovered that the road to academic prominence was paved with paper, the kind of paper that psychiatric journals are printed on, and he was proceeding at a fast pace on that highway to scientific distinction.

Psychiatric research has long been a fashionable thing, and any ambitious fellow with proper university credentials usually can get large grants of money for investigative research projects to start him on the way to becoming a Great Man. Once he has become an "established investigator," it is not too difficult to get his grants renewed every two to three years and to become a hardy perennial in the lush gardens of psychiatric inquiry. The philanthropic foundations and the federal government (mainly through the National Institutes of Health) have large amounts of money earmarked for psychiatric research, and the people who hand out the money rarely inquire minutely about what is done with it ("We must give the investigator complete freedom of action"). A yearly two-hundred-page report, replete with graphs, charts, and diagrams, keeps them happy. Moreover, the granters usually are not experts in the fields they are funding, and consequently they do not know whether the investigators are creative explorers who are doing original work or shams who are merely grinding out balderdash that will hoist them to the top of the academic pile as quickly as possible.

The technical consultants, who advise foundations and government agencies on projects, usually are the colleagues, friends, former students or former teachers of the "established" investigators, and they do not rock the boat. Also, after financing an investigator with six-figure grants for five to ten years, foundation and government administrators are loath to admit to their governing bodies that they have wasted all that money, and so a tacit conspiracy is formed between the granters and the grantees to protect each other. The granters praise the "discoveries and contributions" of the grantees, and the grantees praise the "administrative wisdom and foresight" of the granters. This cozy system extends even into the ways in which candidates are proposed and pushed for Nobel prizes; the only man ever granted a Nobel prize for psychiatric work got it for developing a treatment technique that fifteen years later was generally conceded to be not only useless, but highly dangerous to patients.

Dr. Allen was bogus, and I doubt that our chief ever found out. Worse still, I doubt that Dr. Allen ever found out. He actually thought he was expanding the boundaries of scientific knowledge, whereas in reality he was either repeating, with negligible differences in technique or

140

emphasis, work that had already been done or was nit-picking points that were of little or no significance. If he had never hurt anybody, I would be inclined to remember Dr. Allen charitably, and as to the money, a nation that can spend 150 billion dollars to slaughter a million people in Vietnam can hardly be criticized for financing Dr. Allen in his silly projects. However, Dr. Allen sometimes damaged patients badly.

Mr. Schiebrel was one of them. At the time I served my research apprenticeship under Dr. Allen one of his projects was the evaluation of a new drug for sedating patients before electroshock therapy. The project was pointless, since there already were more than twenty similar drugs on the market, and this one differed from the old ones only in an insignificant detail of its chemical structure; this insignificant detail, however, enabled the large pharmaceutical firm, which had synthesized the drug, to patent it, and it hoped to use the drug to enter a market in which it formerly had not been active. The pharmaceutical company generously financed the project, supplied all equipment and medications, and guaranteed that the study would receive wide publicity after its results were published. Also, if Dr. Allen could get the report of this study on the scientific program of a psychiatric convention (as he did), the pharmaceutical firm would pay all expenses of the investigators for attendance at the convention. Half my stipend during the second year of my residency came from money the pharmaceutical company gave Dr. Allen; I plead innocent on the grounds of youth and inexperience.

We collected sixty patients with severe depressions who were to be treated by electroshock therapy. Electroshock therapy was then the accepted treatment for severe depressions, and though slightly dangerous, it was successful in most cases. Subsequent developments have taken

141

almost all the danger out of electroshock treatment and have reduced the amount of it given by more than 75 percent.

Just before each electroshock treatment we intravenously injected the new drug into the patient, and he immediately went to sleep. We took blood-pressure readings, counted the patient's pulse, and meticulously noted various other reactions before, during, and after the treatment. We also drew blood from him before and after the electroshock treatment for four different laboratory tests. We had two nurse anesthetists standing by in case of respiratory emergencies.

Mr. Schiebrel was about number fifty in our series of sixty cases. He was a middle-aged farmer from a rural district about 150 miles distant from our medical center. He came to the hospital accompanied by his obese, gray-haired wife and his son, who operated a lumberyard in a small town near his father's farm. For four months prior to admission to the hospital Mr. Schiebrel had had a severe depression, and his hospitalization was precipitated when he tried to shoot himself. His family doctor sent him to our university medical center ("Might as well get the best there is"), and we gave him eight electroshock treatments. He looked fine after his eighth treatment and was scheduled to have two more. Then his "complication" occurred.

We had had some trouble with the new drug. Occasionally a patient got a spasm of his larynx thirty to sixty seconds after the drug was injected; this clamped off the respiratory tract and prevented breathing. In most instances these laryngeal spasms lasted only about twenty to thirty seconds; then pressure from straining chest and diaphragmatic muscles broke the spasm and the patient breathed normally. On one occasion, however, the nurse anesthetists had had to put a laryngoscope down the patient's throat and

142

thread a rubber tube between his vocal cords to prevent him from suffocating to death. In other instances we had been able to break the patient's laryngospasm by capping a face mask tightly onto him and giving him oxygen by vigorously squeezing the rubber bag attached to the mask. On two occasions I had broken laryngospasms by the crude but effective expedient of giving the patient a couple of hard thumps on his chest. However, the second time I did that Dr. Allen was present and he told me never to do it again. It would not have looked good in the scientific article to say (if indeed it did say everything honestly) that on several occasions patients with laryngospasms had been pounded on the chest by vigorous young psychiatrists.

On the day of his ninth electroshock treatment Mr. Schiebrel came into the treatment room smiling and alert.

"Do I really need any more of these treatments, Doctor?"

"We'll do this one," I said, "and maybe another one. You're doing fine, but we want to make it permanent, don't we?" One of the fundamental principles of psychiatry is to answer a question with a question. Moreover, I could not tell him that for statistical purposes, Dr. Allen wanted each patient to have a minimum of ten treatments.

Dr. Allen, who was present on this particular morning, added a word or two of professorial comfort, and Mr. Schiebrel lay down on the treatment table. I drew from him the requisite amount of blood for the lab tests and then injected the new drug. Mr. Schiebrel quickly went to sleep, and the nurse put the electrodes on his head as two aides bent over him to pin his body and limbs to the table. However, as we finished preparations to give him the treatment, the nurse and I noted that he had stopped breathing. His chest muscles were straining in rhythmic jerks to get air in and out. His larynx had jammed shut. His lips got blue and his face became dull gray. I called for the oxygen mask, and the psychiatric nurse quickly clapped it on his face, twisted the oxygen valve open, and applied strong squeezes to the inflated bag attached to the mask. Between her squeezes, I put pressure on both sides of his chest. We worked at this for about sixty seconds while his lips and fingernails grew purple. When I lifted my fist above his chest to give him one of my therapeutic thumps, Dr. Allen barked, "Dr. Chapman!" I stopped. "The nurse anesthetists can take care of this," he said.

I looked skeptically at the nurse anesthetists, for I had seen them in action before, but I backed away from the table to let them take over. They were pinch-faced, apprehensive young women in starchy white uniforms, and floppy cloth caps covered their ears and hair entirely. They rushed at the patient, tipped his head back, and inserted a laryngoscope down his throat. The junior of the two nurse anesthetists took a narrow, lubricated rubber tube, slid it into the laryngoscope, and tried to push its tip through the thin, tight line where the spastic vocal cords presented a rigid obstacle. She pushed the tube several times, each time with increasing vigor, but it wouldn't pass. "Give me a larger tube," she shouted anxiously to her co-worker, and the other nurse passed it to her. She slipped it into the laryngoscope and began to ram the vocal cords with forceful jabs. The patient was getting bluer, and the jerking movements of his respiratory muscles were weaker.

Everybody was becoming uneasy.

"Let me take over," said the senior nurse anesthetist, and she quickly slid into the space her junior ceded to her.

She took a large-diameter hard rubber tube from the anesthetists' tray and slid it into the laryngoscope. What her junior lacked in skill, she more than made up for in determination. She repeatedly slammed the end of the tube into the vocal cords while Dr. Allen looked on, somewhat

144

frightened, I think, and I felt sick. The psychiatric nurse and the two aides watched in silence. About the tenth jab the tube slipped through the larynx and into the trachea. The tube was immediately fitted to a respiratory bag and the oxygen tank, and in sixty seconds Mr. Schiebrel was pink and breathing well.

"Good," said Dr. Allen. "Now, let's get on with the treatment."

The psychiatric nurse and I stared at him.

"Don't you think we ought to let this one go?" I asked.

"Of course not," he replied. "Minor troubles like this are to be expected when working with a new drug. You simply have to foresee the possibility of such complications and be prepared to cope with them. Besides that, we don't want to break our series."

Wordlessly, the nurse, the aides, and I moved into position, gave the treatment, and drew the posttreatment blood samples from him. In equal silence we gave two more treatments after that. Then Dr. Allen cheerfully thanked us all, said the project would be finished in a couple of weeks, and left, followed by the nurse anesthetists.

"If those damn nurse anesthetists didn't rupture one or both of that man's vocal cords, I'll take you out for a free hamburger at The Pig's Ear," I said to the nurse.

Unhappily, Mr. Schiebrel's troubles were far worse than that. He couldn't talk for three days and spat blood; on the fourth day he could whisper hoarsely. On the fifth day he developed a high fever and began to have chills. The otolaryngologist who had been called to see him had found his vocal cords badly damaged and blood-crusted. He thought the fever was probably caused by infection secondary to trauma to his larynx and trachea, and we started him on penicillin and sulfa tablets. At that time penicillin was still relatively new, and we gave it in shots once every three hours. Mr. Schiebrel's voice grew steadily better during the next few days, but his general condition became much worse.

Chest X rays were taken at three-day intervals, and two weeks after his traumatic electroshock treatment it was clear that he had an expanding abscess in the central part of his chest cavity. The anesthetists had either perforated his larynx or had damaged it so badly that infection had spread from it into his chest. A mediastinal abscess is a grave illness, and it was very dangerous in the 1940's, when antibiotics were at a relatively primitive stage of their development. In a five-hour operation Mr. Schiebrel's anterior chest wall was opened and the abscess was drained.

During the postoperative period his wife spent her days in the hospital lobby waiting for news three times a day about her husband, and stayed at his bedside most of the time after that on the surgical ward to which he had been transferred. His son drove 150 miles two or three times a week to see how his father was doing.

I had to talk to them. Dr. Allen told me that I was not to reveal the true circumstances of the injury to them, but to say that he had developed acute laryngitis, which had spread to his chest. I lied daily to them, as I was instructed to do. Mr. Schiebrel's son shook his head sadly and said, "And he was doing so well before this laryngitis hit him." His wife said, "Well, it's good, I guess, that he was in a university medical center when he happened to get this infection, because here we know he's getting the best possible care."

Three months after his operation Mr. Schiebrel went home. It was difficult to tell whether his depression had returned or he was simply so debilitated that he seemed depressed. When I happened to meet him in the clinic a year later, he was in good condition psychiatrically, but he had not recovered sufficient physical strength to operate his farm. He had rented it and was living in the small town where his son had his lumberyard.

The report of our research project was in due time published in a leading psychiatric journal. My name was third in the list of five authors. Dr. Allen's name was first. The article concluded that the drug was "a satisfactory addition to our armamentarium of medications for pre-shock medications." The report contained two charts and a page-long table of data on the sixty cases. Mr. Schiebrel was not included in the sixty cases; the article stated that "three cases originally intended for this series were not included because, for various reasons, they did not complete the course of treatment, and three other patients were substituted in their places." The medication never achieved wide acceptance and many years ago was removed from the market.

At the time I was released from military service Dr. Allen was research professor at a leading medical school on the East Coast. He wrote me offering an assistant professorship to work under him. I declined. Five years ago, when he was in his late fifties, he died of a heart attack while attending a psychiatric congress in England. He had a two-page obituary, with a full-page photograph, in America's foremost psychiatric journal. At the time of his death he was professor and chairman of the psychiatric department at one of the nation's major medical schools. He wrote more than two hundred papers during his career, was coauthor or editor of six books, and consultant on research grants to several philanthropic foundations and government agencies.

The obituary, which was written by one of his assistants,

said that "in his death America has lost one of its foremost psychiatric investigators." However, in my opinion, he never did any truly original or significant research.

All save one of his books are now out of print, and I doubt that one will be in print five years hence. His two hundred articles are no longer cited in the lists of references at the ends of articles in psychiatric journals.

I occasionally have wondered how many other Mr. Schiebrels gave him a leg up on his way to the top.

It was a few minutes before 3:00. There was one telephone message. A patient who had picked my name out of the Yellow Pages was requesting an appointment. For many years I had accepted only patients referred directly from physicians, and I therefore told Marie to give him Dr. Terrence Jackson's name, office address, and telephone number.

"Are any of the three o'clock appointments here?" I asked.

"Two of them."

"All right."

9

3:00. This is my crud hour for today. It is reserved for ten- or fiften-minute supportive contacts with various kinds of patients—recovered psychotic patients who need a brief evaluation and a prescription renewal every two to three months, chronic neurotics who cannot talk well enough to do psychotherapy but do better if some authoritative person reassures them periodically and keeps them on a harmless medication, and other assorted patients.

"Who's out there, Marie?"

"Mrs. Hagstrom and Mrs. Stewart."

"Send in Mrs. Hagstrom."

In came a hulking, cheerful, garrulous woman of fifty-five, accompanied by her sister, who is ten years younger. They had driven 110 miles to spend ten minutes with me. They came once every four months and had been coming for three years.

We exchanged greetings and sat down.

"Well, how goes the battle?" I asked.

"Still hanging on," said Mrs. Hagstrom.

Her sister nodded and smiled. "She's fine, Doctor."

"Yes," Mrs. Hagstrom said, "I got a job."

"Really," I said, "modeling or making moonshine?"

Much laughter all around.

"I'm working as receptionist and bookkeeper at Agnes

Martin's beauty parlor. She doesn't pay much, but it keeps me out of mischief."

"Great," I said. "What are the hours?"

"Nine to twelve, and one to six. One day a week off. It'll qualify me for Social Security when I'm sixty-five."

"Great," I said. "Still taking our little pill every day?"

"Of course," she answered. Her sister nodded in agreement.

"Okay. Five or ten more years and you can stop, if one of us doesn't die first."

More laughter.

"Need a prescription?"

"No. I still have one I haven't used yet."

"Getting a few things while you're in town today?"

"Anything we can shoplift."

More hilarity. Mrs. Hagstrom is a hail gal well met.

Her sister said, "We have a few things to buy, things we can't get in Manchester."

"Well, just keep up the good work and come back to see me in four months. Make an appointment with Marie as you go out. I need the money."

"The hell you do," said Mrs. Hagstrom. "I'd like to have half your bankroll."

More guffawing.

Mrs. Hagstrom gave me a hearty handshake and they left.

What does all this mean?

Mrs. Hagstrom, like the rest of us, has had her problems. Once there was a Mr. Hagstrom, but he and she were divorced thirty years ago after a brief, childless marriage. Mrs. Hagstrom then lived for many years with her indulgent parents and after their deaths inherited a little property. She did not remarry, but spent twenty-five years in and out of affairs that provided the citizenry of Manchester, Missouri, with ample gossip to fill their

150

leisure hours. However, she didn't hurt anyone badly; she never broke a marriage. In her middle forties she began to drink heavily, and by the time she reached her early fifties she was a severe alcoholic. One morning her sister, a married woman living in the same town, received a call from a motel near Belmont, Missouri, saying that Mrs. Hagstrom had checked into the motel two days previously and was very sick. Her sister went at once and found her in marked delirium tremens. She screamed about the lizards, huge roaches, and rats that were swarming over her motel floor and walls, and she whispered that men were waiting outside to kill her.

Mrs. Hagstrom spent three weeks under my care on the psychiatric ward at St. Catharine's recovering from her delirium tremens and returning to a state of good nutrition. Once her delirium tremens had cleared, she was the life of the party at St. Catharine's; she took over all conversations in the dayroom and kept everybody in stitches. At the beginning of the fourth week I called her sister to meet me at the hospital one morning, and the three of us had a conference in Mrs. Hagstrom's room. I gave them my sales talk on disulfiram treatment.

I told them that Mrs. Hagstrom had had a serious illness, that delirium tremens is not to be shrugged off lightly as "a touch of the shakes, or the DT's." In various medical research studies it has a mortality rate that runs from 3 to 10 percent. I had two of them die on my hands in the emergency room when I was an intern in a large charity hospital (cases of delirium tremens seen in such hospitals often are brought for treatment only after they have been sick for several days or more). I told them that if Mrs. Hagstrom returned to her drinking, she had a high risk of having more delirium tremens in time, and that occasionally alcoholics had long-lasting psychotic illnesses with many weeks or months of hallucinations, delusions, and panic. I painted all this grimly and accurately. This is one of the few situations in psychiatric practice in which I feel that it is justified to try to frighten the patient into treatment.

I then went into my disulfiram pitch. Disulfiram was discovered by two Danish pharmaceutical chemists in 1949, and it has a peculiar property. A person who takes a small dose of this drug each day notices no effects unless he drinks alcohol. If he drinks even a small amount of alcohol, he becomes very sick in about fifteen minutes. He has headache, weakness, a suffocating feeling in his chest, flushing of the face, generalized muscular pains, nausea, and vomiting. Disulfiram can thus serve as a chemical barrier to drinking.

If a patient accepts disulfiram treatment, he receives a standard dose of it in tablet form each day for seven days, preferably in a hospital, and on the eighth day he receives a small test dose of alcohol to prove to him that this regimen is not a bluff that his relatives and the doctor have concocted. After drinking the test dose (an ounce of whiskey mixed with water), he gets mildly sick and occasionally needs an injection of an antishock drug to raise his blood pressure if it drops too low. (A person on disulfiram who rapidly gulps down half a bottle or less of whiskey in fifteen to twenty minutes can kill himself; such fatalities are very rare, however.) After the effects of the patient's test dose of alcohol wear off in a couple of hours, he remains weak for several hours more. He leaves the hospital the next day, with instructions to him and his relatives that he is to take half a tablet of disulfiram each day for the next five to ten years.

One point is important. Responsibility for taking the medication is not left in the hands of the patient. If it is left

152

up to him, he rarely persists in taking it each day, and after being off disulfiram for fourteen days he can begin to drink again. The administration of disulfiram must be put in the hands of a close relative who once each day, preferably at a set, standard time, gives the patient the half tablet and watches him swallow it. Mrs. Hagstrom lives alone. Hence, her sister each morning drives two miles to her house and gives her the drug.

Since going on disulfiram, Mrs. Hagstrom has become a respectable member of her community. She has repented her sins and is a member in good standing of the Manchester First Methodist Church.

But if disulfiram is so good, why are there eight million alcoholics in the United States? It is because the treatment works only if the patient is highly motivated to stop drinking. Of every eight alcoholics to whom I propose disulfiram treatment, one accepts. Of those who accept, about two-thirds stay on the drug and permanently abstain from alcohol. I have about twenty patients like Mrs. Hagstrom; they come to see me once every four months, since they should maintain at least a loose contact with the physician who is prescribing the medication. Most textbooks of psychiatry state that patients who take disulfiram should enter psychotherapy to solve the underlying problems that caused them to drink, but in many years of using disulfiram I have had only one patient who was interested in psychotherapy once his drinking problem was solved.

The results of both individual psychotherapy and group psychotherapy with alcoholics are very poor. In more than a quarter century in psychiatry I have helped a few people with minor drinking problems by psychotherapy, but I have never successfully treated a severe alcoholic by psychotherapy alone. Most of my colleagues have had similar experiences. A sizable minority of severe alcoholics, however, stop drinking because of nonmedical factors. Alcoholics Anonymous helps a small percentage of them, and others stop drinking because of religious persuasion, marital crises, car smashups while drunk, impending severe liver disease, and other life crises. However, the only medical procedure that in the long run gives better results than the nonmedical ("spontaneous") recovery rate is disulfiram treatment.

Many patients who go on disulfiram subsequently solve the marital, social, and vocational problems that their alcoholism was causing. Others do not. I recall a glib, charming woman in her early thirties who stopped drinking on disulfiram, but continued her pattern of flamboyant, home-wrecking fornication while living with her elderly, well-to-do father, who supported her. In psychotherapy she talked engagingly about her life, but lied so much about her past and present experiences and arrived late for so many appointments that in time we gave it up. Her father came in one day to pay her long-overdue bill and asked to see me. "Doctor," he said, "you cured her of her drinking. Now, do you have a pill for the rest of her?"

3:10. Mrs. Stewart comes in. She is a plump, pleasant young woman with two small children and a good husband in Parkville, Missouri, an old suburb of Kansas City. Since her early adolescence Mrs. Stewart has had various minor phobias and obsessive fears that fluctuate in intensity from one month to the next. In an interview she can talk about her symptoms, and nothing else, for five minutes. Upon inquiry, she invariably reports that all relationships in her life are, and always have been, "fine" and that everybody and everything are "fine"; her shield of bland, protective optimism cannot, and perhaps should not, be shattered.

154

This gives a psychiatrist very little to work with. Psychotherapy is impossible for her; when she first saw me four years ago, I tried it for a couple of months.

As illustrated and discussed during my hour with Mrs. Demarest earlier this afternoon, 80 to 90 percent of the patients seen in general psychiatric work can engage in useful interviews only if the therapist liberally employs questions and comments. However, of even that 80 to 90 percent of patients, a significant number can sustain meaningful sessions for only a month or two before lapsing into silence, repetition, or chatty irrelevance. To these patients the psychiatrist can offer only supportive, brief counseling sessions, if both the patient and the therapist feel they will be useful. In such counseling the therapist gives much reassurance, explains symptoms on the basis of obvious current and past tensions in the patient's life, offers advice on day-to-day problems, and regulates small doses of medications.

Only about 10 percent (and that figure may be high) of the patients encountered in general psychiatric work could talk well enough to engage in classical, on-the-couch psychoanalysis, and only one-fifth or less of that 10 percent could afford it. (As mentioned earlier, these figures are significantly higher in some sophisticated, well-to-do social groups, as contrasted with the public in general.) On-the-couch psychoanalysis probably embraces no more than 2 percent of all psychiatric work done in the United States.

What does a psychiatrist, therefore, do with a woman like Mrs. Stewart?

She pulls out her list, which covers her fearful thoughts and phobias of the last three months. She has about half a dozen items. She runs through them. On December 12 she felt afraid of dying, but she repeated to herself that Dr.

155

Chapman had told her she had no more chance of dying than any other twenty-seven-year-old Parkville housewife. So she wrote this fear down on her list to tell Dr. Chapman the next time she saw him, and forgot about it. On January 3 she felt afraid to leave her house. So she put that on her list; she then took half a tranquilizer tablet (which could have only placebo, not pharmacological, effect) and went shopping. She goes on reading her entries and making a few comments after each of them. When she gets done, I rattle through the reassurances and slogans I've given her every three months for four years. I tell her to continue to write every little worry and fear she has on her "Dr. Chapman list" and then to forget about it. My tone of voice and authoritative manner are probably more important than what I say. If I said it in Latin, it probably would have almost the same effect.

Mrs. Stewart smiles. She says she's doing fine, and she thanks me. I tell her to make another appointment with Marie for three months later. She goes out.

This is supportive psychotherapy reduced to its lowest common denominator. Sometimes I ask myself if I'm exploiting Mrs. Stewart. I think not. I could get along quite well without the small amount of money she pays me each year, and for that sum she is a much more comfortable woman. Anticonvulsant medications free many epileptics of seizures for decades, but cure none of them. Does that mean we should throw away anticonvulsant medications? Not until something better comes along.

3:25. Don Schafer and his mother and father come in. This is a grim story with an uncertain, probably sad ending in the future. Mr. Schafer is a maintenance man in a small pumping station of the Great Western Gas Company. They live near Martindale, a small town fifty miles south of

156

Kansas City, on a forty-five-acre farm, and between the farm and Mr. Schafer's job with the gas company, they get along well. Mrs. Schafer is a motherly woman in a simple print dress and a brown coat. They are devout Baptists.

After they were married nine years and had no children, they decided to adopt one. They came to a Baptist orphanage near Kansas City and there they found Don. He had been brought to the orphanage three weeks previously by welfare workers who had found him abandoned in a cheap boardinghouse; he had been beaten and was malnourished. At ten months he was a mute, motionless infant with staring, vacant eyes, a child who had been badly damaged emotionally. The Schafers felt sorry for him and took him home.

With the mothering of Mrs. Schafer and the fatherly comradeship of Mr. Schafer he slowly came out of his state of frightened isolation. By the age of three he was a shy but affectionate child. He grew into a tall, husky boy, but he was ill at ease with people and, except for school and church, rarely left the Schafers' farm. He got average marks in school and liked to work on the farm. They were fond of him.

When he was sixteen, he went during the summer to work for Mr. Schafer's brother for three weeks, crop spraying on a farm in a nearby county. It was the first time he had ever been away from home overnight. After ten days they received a call from Mr. Schafer's brother, saying that something had happened to Don. "What?" "Well, he's pretty nervous and mixed up." They went at once and found Don in a bewildered, panicky state. He talked about the "ganfelts" and the "big boots" that were after him and the voices that said ugly sexual things about him.

The Schafers' family doctor referred them to me, and with six weeks of treatment at St. Catharine's he emerged

157

from his schizophrenic illness. Mr. Schafer suggested that Don's illness was caused by intoxication by insecticide dust, and at his urging I put the diagnosis "organic brain syndrome associated with chemical intoxication" on their hospitalization insurance forms. This did not affect the benefits the insurance company paid and it made the Schafers feel better.

I saw Don for a year in follow-up visits and kept him on maintenance doses of an antipsychotic medication. He could not engage in psychotherapy; even the most superficial talk about himself scared him badly and had more risk of loosening his weak grip on reality than of helping him.

Then one night I got a call from the emergency room of St. Catharine's. The Schafers had driven up with Don that night. By phone I spoke with Mr. Schafer and with the nurse on duty. Three days previously he had relapsed into another schizophrenic psychosis.

That was two years ago. Since then Don has been hospitalized five times. His periods of improvement are getting shorter and weaker. The Schafers today tell me how much better Don is, how he really knows how to handle livestock on the farm, and how, with Mr. Schafer beside him, he drove the pickup truck to the feed store to pick up a load of feed.

Don may get better. I've seen patients like him recover and stay well. However, the odds are very much against him. He was severely traumatized emotionally in his early life and was a shy, awkward boy before he became ill. Once he arrived in mid-adolescence and began to face the prospect of even minor independence from the Schafers he retreated into a world of delusional withdrawal from reality. During the last three years he has been schizophrenic half the time and during the other half has made a marginal social adjustment. In three more years or less Don probably will be chronically institutionalized in a state hospital. I haven't told the Schafers yet. They're not ready for it.

Don does not look good today. He stares around the room distractedly while the Schafers tell me how well he's doing. Don chimes in with "yup" and "nope" in answers to his parents' cued questions. I raise his dosage of antipsychotic medication a little and tell the Schafers that they can always call me anytime if Don gets upset about something. I tell them to keep Don busy on the farm and make an appointment with Marie to return in thirty days as they leave. Mr. Schafer waits until his wife and Don are at Marie's desk in the waiting room.

"He'll be all right, won't he, Doc?" he asks in a whisper.

"With a little luck we'll make it," I reply. He winks, smiles, and leaves.

I lied to him.

What would you do?

3:40. Wilbur McClintock comes in. After tragedy comes the comic relief. Wilbur is a round-faced, grinning man of forty-five who is married to a former prostitute, and he worries about his sexual potency. Therein lies a tale.

Fifteen years ago Wilbur was running a bar in a mixed black and white district on the East Side of Kansas City. A good-looking black call girl sometimes came into his bar during the slow afternoon hours. He gave her a drink and they talked. When business picked up in the late afternoon, she left. Wilbur catered to workingmen who had a quick drink on the way home from work, and barflies didn't fit into the picture during rush hours. The men drank too much and got into fights over them, and that brought the police in. Three or four such visits from the police were followed by cancellation of a bar's liquor license.

Wilbur liked the call girl; often he just talked with her

over the counter or they watched television together, and he never charged her for the drinks. He was unmarried, and sometimes the girl smiled and they went to a back room and had sex. Then one day Wilbur couldn't get an erection with her. She said he was tired and that they'd do it again another day. They tried it on several other days, but Wilbur was impotent each time. Wilbur became very frightened.

He looked for a psychiatrist in the Yellow Pages, picked out Dr. Warren, and went to see him. At that time Dr. Warren was eighty-eight years old. Dr. Warren had been a general practitioner in Kansas, but in the late 1920's he went to work for a small private psychiatric sanatorium near Kansas City. After a few years there he went into private practice in Kansas City.

By the late 1930's he was a wealthy man, but not from psychiatry. Many years previously he had bought a farm in southern Kansas. He hung onto it long after oil had been discovered on all the surrounding farms. He finally sold it for two million dollars and put the money into gilt-edge securities. In middle age, having been a childless widower for several years, he married his secretary, who was much younger than him. For nine months each year they lived in a large apartment in midtown Kansas City, and for the three summer months they went fishing on an island on which they owned a cottage in Wisconsin.

Dr. Warren kept his office open several hours a day, saw patients for half-hour sessions, and charged them ten dollars. By the time he reached his early eighties all the physicians of Dr. Warren's generation were dead or senile. By asking around, I discovered that no actively practicing psychiatrist in Kansas City had ever met him, though one or two had talked to him briefly on the telephone to get information about patients he formerly had treated. So I went to see him one day. His office was decorated much as it probably had been when he opened it in the 1920's. The

160

waiting room had wicker chairs, faded Maxfield Parrish lithographs in simple frames on the walls, and a worn, dusty rug.

When I walked in, there was no one in the waiting room. I coughed and made various other noises until a middle-aged woman came from a dark corridor; I could hear a television set going full blast in a room at the end of it. I told her (she was both his receptionist and wife, introducing herself as Mrs. Warren) who I was and that I had dropped by briefly to meet Dr. Warren. She disappeared into the dark corridor, and a moment later a chipper man in rolled-up shirt sleeves trotted out. He looked twenty-five years younger than he was. We chatted for fifteen minutes. He talked of doctors who had been dead for thirty years as if they were contemporaries, but he was not senile. He knew who I was, knew the title of a book I had written, and thanked me for the visit. However, he clearly was anxious to get back to his television program, and I soon left. Five years later I saw a notice in the local medical society's twice-monthly bulletin announcing his death at the age of ninety-three. He kept his small practice until a few months before his death.

When Wilbur went to see Dr. Warren, Dr. Warren asked him what his trouble was. Dr. Warren then launched into a twenty-five-minute discourse on bonefishing. He showed Wilbur pictures of his summer cottage in Wisconsin and some of the fish he had caught. Then he got up and said, "As for that other problem, you'll be all right. Come back and see me again in three or four weeks." Wilbur went out. When he got onto the street, he suddenly realized that he hadn't discussed the fee with Dr. Warren. He went back in and, after a bit of shouting down the dark corridor, found the receptionist. "I forgot to pay," he said. "How much is it?" "Ten dollars." He paid her ten dollars and left. He went back to his bar and the next day had successful sexual

161

relations with the call girl. He had no more trouble with impotence.

Four weeks later he went back to Dr. Warren and had another session, which was exactly the same as the first one. Six months of this went by, and Wilbur became convinced that his potency was in some way related to regular visits to Dr. Warren. At ten dollars a month he figured it was worth it.

Then one June day he went to see Dr. Warren and the office was closed. There was a notice on the door: "Dr. Warren will be back on September 15." He had gone fishing on his island in Wisconsin. Wilbur was terrified. He ran for the Yellow Pages and chose my name. When he called, he said that Dr. Warren had referred him to me, and so Marie gave him an appointment.

I listened to the story of his problem, but I did not ask him about the details of his treatment with Dr. Warren. For three sessions I tried to do psychotherapy with Wilbur. It was a failure. He couldn't talk about anything except how worried he was about his potency. At the beginning of the fourth session he got very upset and said he wished Dr. Warren was back.

So I asked him how Dr. Warren had treated him, and he told me. I knew nothing about bonefishing. In fact, I had no idea how bones and fishing could possibly be related.

I sat back in my chair and threw my clipboard and notes onto my desk. "Wilbur," I said, "how's the bar business these days?" For twenty minutes we talked about the ups and downs of running a cheap bar on the East Side of Kansas City. Then I got up and slapped him on the back. "You'll be all right," I said. "Make an appointment with Marie to come back in four weeks."

He grinned, put a ten-dollar bill on my desk, thanked me, and walked out. In four weeks he returned and said he was fine. Since that time he has come every month for a

162

ten-minute session, and he gets very upset if I suggest that we make it once every two or three months. He always lays a ten-dollar bill on my desk. I once asked him why. He said that he felt that the treatment wouldn't work unless he paid each time.

So how did Wilbur happen to marry a prostitute?

One day a rare bird walked into his bar—a Jewish prostitute, Selma Levine, age eighteen. Two years previously she had run away from some kind of horrible home life in Brooklyn and had drifted about the Midwest, working briefly as a waitress and then as a prostitute. She was sick and weak when she landed in Wilbur's bar. She asked for a bourbon and Wilbur poured it for her. She drank it and laid her head on the counter. Wilbur didn't know what to do with her.

His rush hour was coming on, and so he put her on a cot in the back room. When his two fortyish barmaids came in at five to work until closing time, he told one of them to go back and see what she could do for Selma. She returned and said that Selma had abdominal pain, chills, and fever. Wilbur gave the barmaid a five-dollar bill and told her to go to the drugstore across the street and ask the druggist what to give her. The druggist, a friend of Wilbur's, came over to look at her.

"PID," he said.

"What's that?"

"Pelvic inflammatory disease. She's a whore and she's picked up an infection in her tubes and ovaries. She ought to go to the General Hospital, but she says she won't go."

"Then what the hell am I to do with her?"

"Damned if I know."

"Well, you ought to know what's good for this."

"I can give her a lot of penicillin and sulfa pills."

"Will that fix her up?"

"Probably."

"Well, give her the pills. Do you need a doctor's prescription?"

"I'll fix it."

Selma stayed for ten days in Wilbur's back room. She got well, put on weight, and emerged a pretty, black-haired adolescent girl. Wilbur did not have sex with her. He had his code.

When Wilbur told her that it was time for her to move on, she began to cry. She said she had nowhere to go and didn't want to go back to her old life. At closing time she was still crying in the back room of the bar. Wilbur told her to put on her jacket, and he took her home. He lived alone in a neat bungalow in a working-class district. "You can stay here for a while, I guess. Tell the woman who comes in twice a week to clean that she doesn't have to come back until I call her."

Seven months later they married. They now have two black-haired, alert kids. When the muggings got too bad in the neighborhood in which his bar was located, Wilbur closed it, opened a health-food store on the South Side of Kansas City, and moved to a new home near it. Though he has only an eighth-grade education, Wilbur is a quick study. The store is successful. Selma helps him during rush hours on Fridays and Saturdays.

Somewhere in Brooklyn many years ago the Kaddish death prayers (which orthodox Jews say for an apostate) were said for Selma Levine.

Selma McClintock is alive and well in Kansas City.

3:45. I'm running behind and gave Wilbur short shrift today. It makes no difference. I told him I have sick people to see and to get along. He laughed, said he was "just fine," put down his ten-dollar bill, and left.

I went to the waiting room and saw Mrs. Barton. I nodded and she came in.

Mrs. Barton was having a hassle with the Wilton City Board of Education. Wilton City is a small farming village that, much against its will, is in the process of becoming a suburb of Kansas City. Businessmen, lawyers, sales executives, and other invaders are buying up old houses and remodeling them into suburban residences, and vacant lots are sprouting attractive duplexes. For three years the town fathers have been locked in earnest battle with a development company that wants to rezone a farm and put up a shopping center and two hundred houses.

Mrs. Barton's husband is an executive in a stock brokerage firm, and to the old Wilton City residents, the Bartons are some of the intruders who are trying to gobble up their town and turn it into one more anonymous suburb in the patchwork of more than forty municipalities that make up the Greater Kansas City area. The animosity between the old guard and the new residents in Wilton City was affecting what should be done with the Barton's son Gary, one of their three vigorous children.

Gary had seemed quite all right until, at the age of six, he had entered the first grade of the Wilton City Grade School. He could not learn to read. He couldn't tell the difference between a "b" and a "d," he thought "saw" and "was" were the same word, and he persisted in reading "on" as "no" and "no" as "on." His writing, after one year of grade school, consisted of illegible arabesques that he crowded into the upper right-hand corner of a sheet of paper. He flunked the first grade; in the space on his report card where "Promoted to Grade Two" was customarily written, the teacher wrote, "Must Repeat Grade One," and the principal countersigned it.

Mrs. Barton had been to the school a few times during the year and had been dismayed by the forty-two other children in Gary's class and the gray-haired teacher who did not have much time to talk to her. However, Mrs. Barton had been too busy remodeling her new house to give Gary's school situation much attention. Gary's failure jolted Mr. and Mrs. Barton, and they went at once to see the teacher.

The teacher was clearing out her desk and tidying up her records before she began her summer vacation the next day. The interview between her and the Bartons quickly deteriorated into a donnybrook as animosity between the old guard of Wilton City, of whom the teacher was a member, and the well-to-do invaders, of whom the Bartons were conspicuous examples, surfaced.

"The boy unfortunately is somewhat mentally retarded," the teacher declared. "This sort of thing happens. I know it's unpleasant for you, but into each life a little rain must fall." However, her general manner did not seem to indicate much distress over the fact that this particular rain was falling on the Bartons.

"The boy was perfectly all right before he entered this school," Mr. Barton said.

"Parents always have difficulty facing these things, especially when they're the ambitious sort," the teacher snapped back.

For a moment the Bartons held their tempers.

"Do you think it's possible that the fact that there were forty-two other children in the class, and that when the boiler broke in February there was little heat in this building for six weeks, and that there were other problems here may have influenced his inability to learn?" Mrs. Barton asked.

The interview soon became a brawl, in which the teacher cited her thirty-five years of teaching experience, and the fact that only Gary and one other child had failed, and if people were not satisfied with the educational facilities they could go back where they came from, while the phrases "hick town school" and "nineteenth-century

166

methods" escaped the lips of Mr. Barton. The Bartons capped it by pointing out that the boy had not even had an IQ test, to which the teacher replied that they were perfectly free to throw their money away on such things if they wanted to, but that the situation was already clear enough.

The Bartons, furious, hauled Gary off to a psychologist, who found an IQ of 123, in the superior range. At the beginning of the next school year the Bartons had another conference with the teacher, which the principal, a woman in her sixties, attended. The IQ report was triumphantly produced and duly perused by the teacher and the principal. "Good," said the teacher. "Let's hope he settles down and does some work this year." The principal muttered something about "home influences," and the interview ended before it had time to degenerate into another fight.

During the first several months in which Gary, now seven, was repeating the first year of grade school, his parents tutored him each night. They discovered a lot of puzzling things. No matter how many times they went over it with him, he still couldn't distinguish "b's" and "d's," confused "was" with "saw" and vice versa, and was unable to make out the meanings of many words. Moreover, if left alone, he usually started to write in the upper right-hand corner of the page or in the upper center of the sheet; from these points his writing drifted downward and sometimes to the left. Only by sitting at his elbow and continually coaching him could they get him to write from left to right. When he wrote block letters, he usually printed an F as ꟼ and an E as Ǝ, and when he drew a picture of a dog it always pointed its nose in the direction opposite to that of the dog he was copying; occasionally he drew the dog upside down. By Christmas he had made little progress and was again flunking the first grade. In January they took him to their pediatrician, who sent them to me.

I listened to Gary's mother tell this story, and in his mother's presence I examined him. I asked him to write some block letters of the alphabet on a blank sheet of paper. He crowded the first letters into the upper right-hand corner, spread the following ones slowly leftward and downward, and reversed the forms of many of them. I showed him a simple drawing of a bird and asked him to draw it on another sheet of paper; he drew it reasonably well for a boy of his age, but the sample bird pointed its beak to the right and the bird he drew pointed its beak to the left.

I then asked him to stand up and pretend to kick a ball. He kicked with his left foot, though he had written and drawn with his right hand. I rolled a sheet of paper into a tube about one inch in diameter and fastened it with cellophane tape. I told him to pretend it was a telescope and to look through it. He picked it up with his right hand and put it to his left eye.

I took a piece of carbon paper and put it on my desk with the inked side uppermost. Then I placed a sheet of blank paper on top of the carbon paper and wrote on it in block letters, "Run, Spot, run. Dick and Jane saw the cat. The cat played with the ball." I picked up the paper, turned it over, and inspected the hieroglyphics the carbon paper had left on it. I showed it to Gary, and to his mother's surprise, he at once read the sentences without error.

After that I showed the carbon-paper tracings to his mother, who could make out the words only with great effort even after having heard Gary read them once. I took a small hand mirror from the bookcase beside my desk and had Mrs. Barton hold it in front of her face. I went behind her chair and put the sheet with the carbon-paper tracings

168

in such a position that she could see them in the mirror. To her astonishment, she now could read the sentences well.

I then explained to her that Gary was of good intelligence, but that he suffered from strephosymbolia, a condition first described by an Iowa psychologist in the 1930's. He derived the term "strephosymbolia" from the Greek words meaning the *twisting* of *symbols*. This condition is also called "specific learning disturbance," "specific reading disability," and other things. It is fairly common; I see one or two new cases each year.

For unknown reasons, virtually all strephosymbolics are boys. The diagnosis is often missed, and the children are considered to be somewhat mentally retarded or to have emotionally caused learning blocks. I have seen strephosymbolic boys in their late adolescence who had never been correctly identified; some had dropped out of school after the age of sixteen, and others were struggling through high school or college or even postgraduate school despite painfully slow reading and scarcely legible penmanship. One was a medical student who never before had known why, despite long, intense studying, he was always in the bottom third of his class.

These children see everything in a mirror-image way; that is, they see all things as if they were reflected back from a mirror. This does not cause them trouble until they try to deal with the intricate symbols and forms used in reading, writing, arithmetic, and drawing. They write from right to left, reverse the forms of letters, cannot distinguish "b's" from "d's" (since they are mirror-images of each other), and reverse the order of letters in words such as "was" and "saw."

In many cases neither side of the body is dominant in physical dexterity; that is, they are neither entirely right-handed nor left-handed. For example, a strephosymbolic child may eat with his left hand, write with his right hand, kick a ball with his right foot, and look through a microscope with his left eye. Most normal people have all these skilled actions located on one side or the other. If undiagnosed, most of these children eventually learn to read after failing two or three grades in grade school, and they develop the ability to write in a crude manner. In adolescence and early adulthood, if they continue their education, they remain poor or mediocre students despite good intelligence. Extremely slow reading is their main handicap.

What causes this condition? When it was first discovered in the 1930's, a large number of strephosymbolics were left-handed children who had been forced by their parents or teachers to become right-handed. However, during the 1940's and 1950's parents and teachers were thoroughly indoctrinated not to change children's handedness, and in the 1960's and 1970's we have rarely seen children with this history. There now are various theories about what produces this difficulty, but all of them are speculative. We simply don't know.

It is customary to say that strephosymbolics suffer from "mixed cerebral dominance"; that phrase requires a bit of explaining. In almost all people one side of the brain is dominant over the other. In a right-handed person the left half of the brain is dominant, and in a left-handed person the right half is dominant (the nerve fibers descending from the brain into the spinal cord cross to the opposite side low in the brain, so that the dominant left half of the brain of a right-handed person gives him special dexterity in his right hand and right foot and vice versa). Moreover, the brain centers that control speech, reading, writing, arithmetical calculation, and similar skills are, in virtually all people, localized entirely in the dominant half of the brain. Thus,

170

the centers for speech, reading, and other such skills are in the left half of the brain of a right-handed person and in the right brain half of a left-handed individual. If a right-handed person in his old age gets a stroke in the left half of his brain or damages it in an automobile accident during his early adulthood, he may lose his ability to talk, read, write, and carry out other skills involving symbols; a similar injury to the right side of his brain would cause paralyses in his body, but would not affect speech, reading, writing, and other symbolic functions.

In a small number of people, such as Gary Barton, clear dominance of one side of the brain over the other is not established. The two sides exist in uneasy competition with each other. Such a person may eat with his right hand and write with his left one; he uses a screwdriver with his left hand and catches a baseball with his right one. He is similarly erratic in skilled activities with his feet (kicking a ball) and eyes (looking through a microscope).

There is only one clue as to why some people with confused (that is, mixed) cerebral dominance see everything as if it were reflected back from a mirror. If a brain is cut down its center into two equal halves, on a plane that runs more or less from the nose to the back of the neck, both the right and left halves of the brain are anatomically identical in every respect but one. The left and right halves are mirror images of each other. That is, in every millimeter of its immensely complex structure, throughout its entire depth, the right half of the brain is what the left half of the brain would look like if it were seen reflected back from a mirror. This, however, does not solve the problem; it only increases the mystery.

I had already explained these things to Mr. and Mrs. Barton in a previous session. I had also pointed out to them that there were good methods for correcting this difficulty.

171

With proper schooling by carefully trained teachers, this problem usually was overcome or at least greatly decreased in about a year. Such work was done in a special school run by the Kansas City School Board in central Kansas City; schools from outlying districts could, for a fee, send pupils to this central school for a year or more of special education, after which the children usually returned to their local schools and proceeded with their education in regular classes.

Mrs. Barton had come to my office this afternoon to get a three-page report, with a covering letter to the Wilton City School Board, in which I explained Gary's trouble. The letter emphasized how commonly this condition is overlooked and that it may be difficult to identify; I went out of my way to relieve the teacher and the principal of any responsibility for not detecting Gary's problem, and I expressed my confidence that they would do everything possible to help this interesting pupil. The Bartons were quite willing to pay the fee for the special school for one year and thus avoid a long bureaucratic struggle with the financially strapped Wilton City School Board over an item that was not provided for in their annual budget. However, the Bartons wanted the record set straight so that their son could go back into the Wilton City school system with a clean slate after he had his year of special schooling. Also, they wanted to prepare the ground for Gary in later years to make up for the two years he had lost by attending summer school.

I told Mrs. Barton that I thought, with my report, all this could be arranged without any difficulty.

She looked at me skeptically. "You haven't met those farmers out in Wilton City," she said. "We'll probably end up sending Gary to a private school so he can catch up with children of his own age."

172

"No," I said, "I think it can be worked out with the Wilton City school people. That's why I had you drop by to pick up my report and letter instead of mailing it to you. There are some things that are difficult to say in a letter or to explain on the phone. You see, your pediatrician is Dr. Caruthers, and his father-in-law is Mr. Nunley."

"That man who is mayor of Wilton City?"

"Yes. Have your husband make some photocopies of my report. Then take a copy of my report to Dr. Caruthers and ask him to have his father-in-law talk to the superintendent of schools or perhaps to a member of the school board. About two weeks after that take my report to the school and, almost apologetically, hand it to the teacher and the principal. Then talk about the weather for a couple of minutes. Within a few days they'll arrange everything for you. That's the best way to arrange things in a small town like Wilton City."

She smiled.

I told her that if they had any trouble to call me, but I thought they wouldn't.

There are advantages in practicing psychiatry in the area where you grew up.

Marie came in. She said that Mr. and Mrs. Miller, my 4:00 patients, had not come in yet. I was not surprised. They usually arrived late. Their delay gave me a few minutes for paperwork. I pulled out my notes and dictated onto a tape my report on the compensation case I'd seen that morning for Dan Baum at Mt. Sinai. Marie would type it up the next day. I also caught Terry Jackson between patients and gave him a five-minute rundown on Helen McLaughlin. He thanked me. She had made an appointment to see him the next morning.

Marie brought in a Coke, which I drank from the bottle.

My wife called me. She knows about when to reach me between patients. Had I paid the clothing bill at Reichfeld's for last month? Yes, I was sure I'd paid it. Send it back marked "Already paid." I asked her how everything at home was. Everything was fine.

I told her I'd arrive home late; it was the first Monday of the month, and I had a departmental meeting at St. Catharine's and a staff meeting at Elmdale. I had no other meetings for the rest of the week. The Bethesda Hospital staff meeting was the following week, and the Mt. Sinai departmental meeting was on the third Tuesday of every month.

Okay? Okay. She was a nurse when I married her. She knew what she was getting into.

I hung up, and a moment later the telephone rang again in the outer office. Marie answered it and she buzzed me. I picked up the receiver.

"Dr. Chapman speaking. . . . Oh, hello, Dr. Porter. . . . Yes, I know who you are. You're the young fellow Bill Knight took in out in Independence. If it works out, it ought to be a good thing for both of you. He has a large practice, as I suppose you're finding out. . . . Well, I suppose he'll find more time to do that now. He likes the fishing down there. What's your problem? . . . All right, let me get a sheet of paper here. . . . Did he cut any tendons? . . . Good . . . How do you spell that name? . . . . S-T-E-R-B-I-N-S, Sterbins. Okay. His address? I'll need it in reserving a bed for him. . . . Phone number? . . . The emergency-room secretary there will have it on the record sheet. I'll wait. . . . Okay. Wife's first name? . . . Any telephone number where he works or she works? . . . Has he ever been psychiatrically hospitalized before? . . . Never mind, then. It's not too important at this point. Does he accept the idea of going to a psychiatric

174

hospital? . . . And his wife? . . . All right. That simplifies things. Now, Dr. Porter—by the way, what's your first name? . . . Okay, Ralph, I'm going to arrange everything for you on this patient. Within twenty minutes we'll have him on his way to a psychiatric ward. It will probably be Mt. Sinai, but, if not, it will be St. Catharine's. As a last resort, we always have Elmdale. I'm overloaded, but I'll get the hospital bed and I'll arrange for Terry Jackson to take care of him. He's new in town, and I've sent him a lot of patients, and so far I've had no complaints from the referring physicians or the relatives. Terrence Jackson. He's on the Plaza. What's the number of Independence Baptist? . . . And your extension number? . . . Okay. Stay near that phone, and within ten minutes either Terry or I will call you. Give the patient six hundred milligrams of chlorpromazine right now in capsules or tablets. It makes management of him on the way to the psychiatric ward easier and decreases the risk of another suicidal attempt before he gets there. You'll be hearing from me. . . . Okay. Good-bye."

I hung up and called Mt. Sinai.

"Hello, this is Dr. Chapman. May I have the admission office, please? Thank you. . . . Hello, this is Dr. Chapman. Do you have a bed on psychiatry? . . . Is it for a man or a woman? . . . Fine, I'll take it. The name is Sterbins. S-T-E-R-B-I-N-S. Frank R. 12441 Lansbury Lane, Independence. Home phone number is 888-2655. Wife's name is Nancy. Work phone is the Ford plant in Clay County, extension 614. Age thirty-seven. . . . He must be covered by the same hospitalization policy that covers all Ford employees there. I'll make sure his wife comes with him and drops by your office to sign the admission papers and give all that data. . . . Put him down as a depression. . . . He slashed his wrists, but he's been sutured, and there were no cut tendons. He'll be coming in by ambulance from the emergency room at Independence Baptist, and he's been sedated. Dr. Terrence Jackson will take care of him, but he'll be under my name. . . . I know he's not on the staff yet, but he was approved by the psychiatric department at the last departmental meeting, and it's just a matter of time before he'll be approved at the next general staff meeting. . . . Look, honey, it's all right. I've had a couple of other patients in there under him in the same way. I'll sign the admission forms and countersign the order sheet first thing tomorrow morning and put a progress note on the chart saying that he's taking care of him under my direction. Is that okay? . . . Fine. The patient will be in within an hour or so. You're a doll. Thanks. . . . Good-bye."

After disconnecting, I dialed Mt. Sinai again and asked for the psychiatric ward.

"This is Dr. Chapman. May I speak to the ward secretary, please? . . . Hello, this is Dr. Chapman. Is that Miss Barclay? . . . Okay. Within an hour or so a Mr. Frank Sterbins, S-T-E-R-B-I-N-S, will be arriving there. He's a wrist slasher, but there were no cut tendons, and he's been sutured. He'll arrive by ambulance, and he's been sedated with six hundred milligrams of chlorpromazine. His wife will be with him in the ambulance. They're both cooperative. Terry Jackson will take care of him, but the patient will be under my name. . . . Yes, I'll sign both of them, and I'll put a progress note on the chart saying that Jackson is taking care of him under my supervision. Tell Miss Spitzer all that if she's still there and objects. . . . Oh, she did. . . . Well, this is probably one of the afternoons she goes to have her ego dry-cleaned at her analyst's. It must be nice to be rich. . . . Don't giggle like that, Miss Barclay, or she'll fire you one of these days, even if

176

evening-shift ward secretaries are hard to find. Look, Dr. Jackson will phone all the orders within half an hour and he probably will drop by to see him later on. Tell the patient's wife what kind of clothing he'll need and the rest of it. . . . Thanks a lot. Good-bye."

I then dialed Terry Jackson's number.

"Hello, this is Dr. Chapman. I'd like to speak to Dr. Jackson, please. . . . Look, honey, tell him it's Dr. Chapman. Dr. Harry Chapman. I just talked to him about Mrs. McLaughlin ten minutes ago. I'm sending him a fair number of patients, and this one is pressing. He's a wrist slasher who's about to go to Mt. Sinai, and Dr. Jackson is going to take care of him. . . . Well, what kind of patient is it? . . . Is he doing a neurological exam on him? . . . Then you can interrupt him. . . . It will be all right, darling. If he bawls you out, call me and I'll tell him that I insisted. . . . Thanks. . . . Hello, Terry? This is Harry Chapman. Look, I have a patient for you. . . . Ready? . . . The name is Sterbins, S-T-E-R-B-I-N-S, Frank R." I repeat the address, the telephone numbers, and other data. "I've already reserved a bed at Mt. Sinai, and they're expecting him. He's in the emergency room at Independence Baptist." I give him the number and the extension number. "The patient has been sedated with six hundred milligrams of chlorpromazine. The referring doctor is Ralph Porter. He's a good man for you to get to know. He's just gone into practice with Bill Knight out in Independence. They have a large practice and a good one. Bill is an old Independence boy and he takes care of a lot of the local notables out there. Moreover, he doesn't treat a neurotic with hormone shots and tranquilizers for three or four years and then refer him to a psychiatrist when his money runs out. And if he says a patient needs to be in a psychiatric hospital, he's usually right; the patient is either seeing things or just tried to hang himself in the basement. So Ralph Porter is a good connection for you; in ten to fifteen years he'll probably be running the practice while Bill Knight is fishing and golfing somewhere. I've cleared things with the admission office at Mt. Sinai, and the psychiatric ward knows he's coming in. He'll technically be under me, but he's your patient. He'll be just the same as that woman I put in there under you four weeks ago and that other one, that man from Kansas City, Kansas. He'll be coming in by ambulance, and his wife will be with him. Emphasize to them at the emergency room at Independence Baptist that she's not to leave Mt. Sinai until she's talked to the ward secretary on the psychiatric unit and to the girls in the admission office. Porter—his first name is Ralph—called me about ten minutes ago and knows you're going to take care of this case. But he doesn't know which hospital yet. He's waiting for your call at that extension number at Independence Baptist, and he's probably anxious to get back to his office. So call him right away, tell him where to send the patient, get any data I've left out, and tell him how happy you are to know him. Also, if you can make it, it would be a good idea to drop by Mt. Sinai tonight on your way home, and if it's going to be before six, tell the psychiatric ward at Mt. Sinai to have the wife wait to see you. It makes a good impression on the family, and they tell the referring doctor, and everybody's happy. . . . No thanks needed. Only too glad to help. In fact, it's good to have somebody to take these cases I'm too busy to take on. . . . Okay. . . . Good-bye."

This ten-minute chore was not all altruism on my part. I was making a couple of friends—Dr. Ralph Porter and Dr. Terry Jackson. Though I was referring tough cases to Terry, I gave him good pointers on how to take care of them, and I also linked him up with the referring physicians instead of blocking him from them, as Irv Weiner had done to me in

178

my first year of practice. A basic rule in medical practice is: Turn down patients when you must, but always help a referring physician. My father had a saying: A business is built one customer at a time. A medical specialist's practice is built one referring physician at a time.

I was maintaining my contacts with the younger generation of physicians, and that's important. I have seen competent, even distinguished, physicians lose their practices during their sixties and be forced into retirement against their will for lack of patients. Their old patients moved to distant cities or other parts of town, or went to nursing homes, or died, and the referring physicians of their own age group similarly disappeared.

Hence, I'm careful to keep on good terms with the younger doctors. Ralph Porter and Terry Jackson needed me today. Fifteen years from now I may need them, and I know how to ring them up gracefully and let them know that I have more empty hours than I like.

In my family we die at our desks. My father, half blind and somewhat senile, worked six and a half days a week until he was seventy-six, and died at seventy-seven. My mother takes piano lessons, swims, and attends Bible college at the age of eighty-one. My brother could live extravagantly on the income from his gilt-edged investments, but he spends fourteen hours a day, seven days a week, running the largest, most lucrative suburban restaurant in Kansas City, which bears our family name. The rising generation, in their late teens and early twenties, are, each in his own way, much the same.

I couldn't stand retirement. So Dr. Porter and Dr. Jackson may one day be important to me.

10

4:15. Mr. and Mrs. Miller have come for their twice-monthly battle. I wish they hadn't come, which is, to say the least, a somewhat undesirable way for a psychiatrist to feel about his patients.

I go to the door, nod to them, and they enter. She takes up her position in the sofa chair in front of me, and he sits on a wooden chair at her side. I lean back in my swivel chair, cross my left leg over my right knee, and wait for the fireworks to begin.

They are a well-dressed, prosperous-looking couple in their late thirties. They live in an elaborate mobile home in a trailer court on the edge of town. He makes ninety thousand dollars a year selling ball bearings for a German firm, and they have seen psychiatrists in Atlanta, Dallas, San Francisco, Detroit, and Albany. I have reports from most of them in my file on the Millers. They have been married twelve years and are childless.

"Well, how have things been going?" I ask.

"Huh!" he says and glares contemptuously at her.

"Tell him what happened," she challenges him.

"Doctor," he says, "I can't stand it anymore. I've had it up to here." He runs his hand across his gullet. "I can't go on being married to a slut who chases every pair of pants she sees."

Mrs. Miller explodes with shouts and tears. "Slut? I've

never stepped out on him. And I've had plenty of chances. And I ought to. If I'm accused of it night and day, I might as well do it."

"You see what she says, Doctor?" he cries. "She as much as admits it. Hell, if I wanted to marry a whore, I should have married one instead of—"

Mrs. Miller starts screaming. "Shut up. How can I stand that? He calls me worse things than that at home. He yells at me all night long. Last week the manager of the trailer court came and told us that if we don't make less noise, we'll have to move out. The neighbors complain that they can't sleep at night."

Mr. Miller sneers and breaks in. "Throw us out? Bullshit! She knows how to take care of him so he won't throw us out."

Mrs. Miller breaks into a noise that is halfway between a wail and a sob. I am glad that there is no one but Marie in the waiting room.

"Yeah, look at her, Doctor. But she knows it's the truth. I as much as caught her with a trailer-court manager in Cleveland."

"He just came in to collect the rent and I gave him a cup of coffee, and he was sixty-eight years old. Old enough to be my father, and the trailer door was wide open all the time."

He snorts at her, and she moves from the defensive to the attack. "He just accuses me to hide his own running around. I found sex stains on his underwear last week when I did the wash, and sometimes he doesn't come home until eleven or twelve at night. Other women in the court tell me I shouldn't put up with it. Everybody knows about it. And he has sex with me only a couple of times a month. What more proof do I need?"

"Doctor," he appeals to me, "how can I have sex all the time with a woman who rents out her cunt by the hour?"

Mrs. Miller literally howls with rage, and I look at the ceiling. As the noise subsides, I say, "Those are mighty strong words, Mr. Miller. Don't you think a little apology is in order?"

"I apologize," he says in a tone that makes those words sound like an insult.

"Do you know what he did last week? I'll tell you what he did last week. Right after dinner on Tuesday—"

"Monday," he corrects her.

"All right, Monday," she says, scarcely stopping. "Right after dinner he said that he had a business meeting and wouldn't be back until late, maybe midnight, and not to wait up for him. As if I would wait up for him, anyway. So I'm watching television, the *Soul of Darkness* program, if I remember right, when at about eight fifteen he slams open the door and comes charging in. 'Where is he?' he shouts. 'He's here somewhere. Where's he hiding?' As if I could hide anybody in a trailer. He bangs open the bathroom door and goes in and comes out, jerks aside the sliding screen to the bedroom, and runs around like he's off his nut. I think to myself that he's gone completely off his rocker this time. All the time he's shouting, 'Where is the son of a bitch? I'll kill him.' I run and shut the door to the trailer, which he left open, so the neighbors can't hear.

"Then he runs to the dresser drawers and starts throwing the clothing all over the floor, looking for his pistol. I tell him I hid it and he can look all night but he won't find it. It's not safe to leave a loaded pistol around the house with a lunatic like him running wild. He says to tell him or he'll knock me down. I tell him to knock me down, and if he does I'll call the police, and won't that look good at the home office in New York—their star salesman in jail in Kansas City for wife beating. He calls me a horrible name. I'd be ashamed to tell it to you, Doctor."

182

"Tell him, tell him," Mr. Miller shouts. "It's the truth, it's God's own truth."

She disregards this interruption and starts off again at breakneck speed. "So he goes through the whole trailer, throwing all my clothing out of the drawers and closets, cursing and shouting that he'll find the son of a bitch if it's the last thing he does. 'In the drawers and closets?' I ask him. 'Maybe you think I'm having an affair with a midget?'"

She stops, sinks back in the chair, and glares at her spouse.

He waves his hand at her. "You see, Doctor, you see what I have to put up with? Hysterics. It's all lies—"

"Lies?" she screams. "It's the truth, the whole truth, and nothing but the truth."

He looks at the door and makes a guttural noise of disgust.

She attacks again, finding him temporarily inactive. "Then who are all those women who are always calling our number? Just who are they, I'd like to know? His office is in our home, as you know, and so all day long I'm answering the telephone. Women call. I ask what they want. They say they'll call back later. I ask them to leave their numbers. Sometimes they don't. He says they're all the secretaries of his customers, but if they're all the secretaries of his customers, why won't they leave their numbers?"

"Because their bosses are moving around and won't be in their offices by the time I return their calls, you idiot," Mr. Miller yells.

She looks defiantly at him, opens her purse, and pulls out a cigarette. He fishes an expensive lighter out of his pocket and lights it for her. They do this in silence. We're between rounds.

"Thank you," she says in a tone that sounds like "Drop dead."

"Don't mention it," he replies in a snarl that sounds like "The same to you, you bitch."

Then they go into another skirmish, battling every inch of ground, toe-to-toe. However, I am no longer listening to them. With wrinkled brow, in apparent, deceptive concentration on their problems, I am staring at the top of my desk. I am lost in contemplation of KOOB TNEMTNIOPPA. Those golden, magical words lie always before me on my desk, in case I need them. I don't know how I could have tolerated many hours of psychiatric practice without the consolation of KOOB TNEMTNIOPPA (pronounced koob tee-nemt ni-op ah). Without the comfort of these words I could not have survived the interminable complaints of Mrs. Rourke (a psychiatrist's mother), the tedious laments of Mr. Randall, and the endless confusion of Mr. Kahlberg.

I have studied these words in great detail, and their magical influence has a calming effect upon me.

I can tell you many interesting facts about KOOB TNEMTNIOPPA. These two words contain fifteen letters. Fifteen is a significant number. It is divisible by 1, 3, 5, and 15. Moreover, the total of 1, 3, 5, and 15 is 24. Twenty-four is even more mystical than 15, because it is divisible by 1, 2, 3, 4, 6, 8, 12, and 24. A number as low as 24, which is divisible by eight numbers, can mean many things, and their explanation has helped me get through innumerable hours of psychotherapy. Further consideration reveals that 15 plus 24 is 39, which is divisible by 1, 3, 13, and 39. A number that in addition to being divisible by itself is divisible only by 3 and 13 must be approached with caution and respect, for 3 brings good fortune and 13 brings bad luck.

Moreover, the sound of KOOB TNEMTNIOPPA has an enchanting quality. It brings to mind medieval alchemists

184

scrutinizing boiling caldrons of rare metals at midnight hours. It has a hint of witches' curses and warlocks' chants. In more benignant ways, it suggests the protecting incantation of a brown-robed priest or an ancient rabbi who, despite danger to himself, has dared to use these powerful words to ward off malicious goblins or predatory demons.

KOOB TNEMTNIOPPA leads the imagination into dark, dank, stone-arched corridors where red-eyed reptiles scurry across the floor and thick cobwebs pinion the unwary intruder. At other times these eerie words suggest exhortations shouted into the wind from a cliff or parapet to protect a cowering village from impending doom.

KOOB TNEMTNIOPPA can, in gentler moments, be crooned to a sleeping infant prince or hero who will one day lead his people to freedom or give them wise laws and teach them how to live in wealth and harmony. A lover could whisper KOOB TNEMTNIOPPA in his sweetheart's ear, and she could lisp it back to him with a kiss.

KOOB TNEMTNIOPPA also can raise visions of glistening banks of scientific instruments with coded dials, long rows of knobs and levers, and valves whose wavering pointers spell salvation or ruin. Or, KOOB TNEMTNIOPPA might be the name of a new, complex chemical that is distilled, drop by drop, into a flask and promises relief to millions of suffering people who have not yet even heard of it. KOOB TNEMTNIOPPA may hold the key to some missile-guiding computer that has lost its way, or it may be the name of a yet undiscovered planet where impalpable forms of life slither or dance or moan.

Sometimes KOOB TNEMTNIOPPA is arcanely sexual. It may be written over the entrance to an Asiatic harem where one dallies with black-eyed houris in forbidden ways. The Prophet has promised that in paradise each faithful son of Islam will have at his disposal eighty-one soft-fleshed virgins and that each orgasm will last a thousand years. Perhaps our paradise will be similarly provisioned, and KOOB TNEMTNIOPPA is what they utter as they open their lips and spread their bodies to receive the blessed.

KOOB TNEMTNIOPPA is APPOINTMENT BOOK spelled backward.

A shriek from Mrs. Miller jolts me out of contemplation of it.

In response to something Mr. Miller has just said, of which I am oblivious, she is wailing. I stare at her and she becomes silent.

"Perhaps we can look at this from another angle," I say. That is one of the stock phrases I use when patients yank me back from KOOB TNEMTNIOPPA and I don't have the least idea what they have been talking about for the last five to ten minutes.

Mr. Miller leans forward and says earnestly, "Doctor, you probably have wondered many, many times why I put up with a woman like this. Well, I'll tell you why. It's because I know that if I left her, and God knows that I'm tempted to do it every day of my life, she'd go completely and utterly to pieces."

"Hah!" she sneers and starts to say something. But he rushes on before she can get anything out.

"Dr. Binder in Detroit told me that if I left her she'd become a chronic alcoholic and die of the DT's or drugs within two years, and rather than have that on my conscience I've—"

"You liar," she screams, "he never said that at all. In fact, he told me that you are one of the most severe cases of infantile personality he'd ever seen and that I was the only thing that was holding you together. He told me I was a heroine. That was his very word, a heroine. And Dr.

Chapman knows it, because he has Dr. Binder's report in his files."

Mr. Miller throws his head back and shouts at the ceiling, "A heroine! Oh, God, the poor woman is stark, raving mad," and turning from the ceiling to her, "Heroine, my ass."

She draws herself up stiffly in her chair and says to me, "I apologize for my husband's crude expressions, Doctor."

"Oh, balls!" groans Mr. Miller. "Doctor, you should hear her at home. She can outcuss any truck driver between here and San Francisco. And furthermore, I'd like to have a fifty-dollar bill for every time she's threatened to kill me. Haven't you threatened to kill me? Deny that if you can. Just ask her, Doctor, if she hasn't threatened to kill me."

"It was in self-defense," she shrieks.

"Oh, yeah? Then, have I ever threatened to kill you? You just tell me if I've ever threatened to kill you. No! Convicted by your own silence."

Silence is something that neither Mr. nor Mrs. Miller can tolerate being accused of, and she launches into a shrill tirade.

"His own family have told me dozens of times, hundreds of times, that they don't see how I can stand him. His own mother says he's impossible to live with and always has been. His sisters won't have anything to do with him except when they want money from him, and his very own brother has told him that if he ever comes home again, he'll cause both his parents to die of heart attacks. I swear to God that—"

"That's sacrilegious," he cries. "The name of God on her lips is enough to—"

"Then deny that your own family can't stand you," she shouts, refusing to allow him to deflect her from her current line of attack.

187

There is a moment's pause.

He looks at me with resignation. "You see, Doctor," he says quietly, "she's psychotic. It's really pathetic when you stand back and look at it."

"It!" Mrs. Miller shrieks. "He calls me *it*." And she breaks into sobs.

He regards her with a look of august compassion. "She breaks down completely at nothing at all. A mere word, a simple—"

Mrs. Miller's breakdown is brief. She explodes, "Oh, look at him, the hypocrite! Playing the saint, and just yesterday he told me he wished I was dead."

"You lying bitch," he hollers.

"He said it. I swear he said it. He said the world would be better off without people like me."

"You're hallucinating," he retorts. "You're sick." He puts the palms of his hands on his thighs with the fingers pointed inward, leans forward, and shakes his head from side to side, as if to say, "That's the end of the matter."

However, that does not end the matter, for the next instant Mrs. Miller sneers, "Hallucinating? I'm really quite surprised that he can even pronounce the word. He's practically illiterate. He didn't even graduate from high school. He only got his high school certificate by taking that test when he was in the Navy."

"There she goes again, throwing her education at me. And what education, may I ask? A high school diploma, which she probably got by screwing the principal, and six months in typing school."

"Look who's talking, an ignoramus who only knows how to bully weak women and—"

"Weak," he roars. "Deny that you hit me last week. Deny it. Look at my bruise." And he pulls up his shirt and undershirt to reveal a scarcely visible blue mark on the right side of his chest.

188

"You got that when you stumbled against the open bathroom cabinet, you drunken bum," she says.

"But deny that you hit me," he retorts.

"And who hit who first? Just who, I'd like to know?"

There is a momentary lull as he stuffs his shirt and undershirt back into his trousers and she sits staring fixedly in the opposite direction.

I dive in with a question, thinking that I may get them off on a different track for a few minutes: "How's the ball-bearing business?"

"Fine," he says. "No thanks to her." If I asked him about the latest advance in space exploration, he'd somehow turn his reply into an insult to his wife.

"Huh!" retorts his wife. "He wasn't going anywhere in the company until I took over his paperwork and started helping him entertain customers."

"Oh, damn!" her husband says. "It's a miracle I ever sell anything when she keeps me so upset all the time."

And so it went on for the rest of the session. Why do I see the Millers? Because they need it. They both are insecure, immature people who cannot form close interpersonal relationships with anyone. I have fifty-four photocopied pages of reports from their previous psychiatrists and clinical psychologists explaining how they got this way, but no therapist has ever changed them. Neither one is capable of love and intimacy with another person, and the only level on which they can maintain a vibrant relationship is a chronic brawl.

Half a dozen psychiatrists have told them they cannot help them, and twice I have discharged them with advice that they fight it out alone or get a divorce. Within a few days they call back for more appointments. Psychotherapy with either one separately is impossible. Each spends fifteen minutes blaming everything on the other and then has nothing more to say.

Without each other they would be lost. He probably would become an alcoholic and she would flounder in and out of several marriages and divorces. They separate at least two or three times a year. He sleeps in a motel for a few nights, and then, on some pretext, they are back together again.

However, all this must have some kind of sanction. Someone must supervise it, regulate it, and give it an aura of respectability. You can't scream at your husband or your wife into the small hours of the night two or three times a week unless there is some plausible rationalization for it. Their rationalization is that *the other one* "is in treatment." That is how this circus is explained to neighbors or anyone else who becomes aware of it.

Also, they need each other in other ways. Mrs. Miller has become used to living on ninety thousand dollars a year, and dropping back to a sixth of that on her own or with another husband would be difficult. Furthermore, she is a valuable asset to her husband in his business. He's a top salesman, but he has no patience with paperwork and correspondence. After ten minutes of trying to fill out reports and write letters, he starts to curse and throw papers around the room. Hence, she does all the paperwork, and she knows almost as much about the ball-bearing business as he does. He can't handle the correspondence and she can't walk into an office and sell half a million dollars' worth of ball bearings.

Moreover, she helps him in entertaining customers. Two or three nights a week they take purchasing agents, consulting engineers, business executives and their wives out to dinner. For three or four hours the Millers can pull themselves together and present the picture of a charming, devoted couple. She carries her share of the conversational load well, and you wouldn't want two nicer people to go out with. They may fight all the way to their guests' doorstep and take the battle up again as soon as the last smiles are exchanged, but they never slip in front of a customer. It's "dear" and "honey" in front of anybody who buys ball bearings.

My wife and I ran into them one night at a plush restaurant, and much to my embarrassment, they insisted that we join them at their table. They wouldn't take no for an answer and presented us to a couple of purchasing agents and their wives. They praised me as the doctor who had patched up "that little spat we had a while back" and looked lovingly at each other and kissed to prove it. A pleasant evening was had by all. When it came time to leave, we discovered that Mr. Miller had already paid our bill, and the manager and the waiter bowed out Mr. and Mrs. Miller and their guests.

When we got home, my wife said, "Mr. Miller said that he and his wife had been your patients. They're such a lovely couple. What kind of trouble could they have had?"

It was late, and I said, "We all have a few problems now and then."

I never discuss my cases with my wife, and on a number of occasions I have come home to find former or current patients seated as guests in my living room. At other times, when my wife or someone else introduces me to one of my patients, whose life history I may know in detail, I accept the introduction without comment. If the patient remarks that he is or has been my patient, I simply say, "Oh, yes." I am somewhat more conservative than most psychiatrists in this respect.

When my father started taking me around on his business calls during my middle adolescence, he told me, "If you meet a man you know, and he's with a woman you don't know, don't talk to him unless he talks to you first." The same rule, somewhat modified, applies to psychiatrists. When you see a patient at a social occasion, it is best not to talk to him unless he talks to you first or indicates plainly that he is going to do so. Otherwise his wife or girlfriend or other companion may inquire, "How does it happen that you know a psychiatrist?" And if he happens to be a homosexual whose wife and children do not know this fact, or a man who has not yet disclosed his three previous marriages to his female companion (or vice versa), or a former schizophrenic or alcoholic who was hospitalized under your care and did not tell this to his employer when he was hired, he may find such a question awkward.

I drink little alcohol because I become talkative when tipsy, and my gossip could injure many people.

It is a few minutes before five. I terminate today's session with the Millers and tell them to make another appointment for two weeks later with Marie as they leave. I'm shortchanging them on time today, but it makes no difference. As they leave, each remarks that he hopes the other will soon begin "to cooperate in the treatment."

Marie comes in and says she'd like to leave early. I reply that it's all right, since the last patient is Mr. Gardner. A physician should never stay alone in his office with a patient of the opposite sex; prudence and professional ethics dictate this. Hence, I agree that after Mr. Gardner comes in, Marie can turn off all but one dim light in the waiting room and set the door to lock automatically behind her as she leaves.

I ask her if there are any calls.

Only one. Dr. Mulvaney's office called to remind me of the departmental meeting at St. Catharine's at 6:15.

"Thank you."

"Good night, Doctor."

"Good night, Marie."

192

11

5:00. Mr. Gardner comes in. He is a tall, gaunt man of fifty-one. He went to work for the telephone company as a lineman in his late adolescence, but in his early twenties he borrowed money from two uncles and bought a swampy meadow in North Kansas City. With the aid of three of his cousins he built two small houses on a corner of the meadow and sold them. With that money he paid off his uncles. He went on working for the telephone company and let anybody who wished dump dirt and debris on his wet meadow. Every three months his brother-in-law went in with a bulldozer and leveled off the mounds of dirt and junk.

Then the exodus of whites from the East Side of Kansas City began, and with it came the building boom in North Kansas City. Real estate developers offered Ed Gardner ten to twenty times what he paid for his meadow, but he clung to it and went on filling it in. When the Greater Kansas City Industrial Corporation offered him eight hundred thousand dollars for it to put in a shopping center, he turned them down, borrowed every dollar he could, and built the shopping center himself. He quit the telephone company and worked side by side with nonunion labor sixteen hours a day; he built his shopping center in eight months and paved the parking lots. He paid off his debts in four years and became a multimillionaire.

However, he hasn't changed his life-style much. He lives in a larger, better house and his car is always new, but he is a deacon in the same Baptist church he has attended since his late twenties, pitches horseshoes and fishes with his boyhood chums, and buys his clothing off the rack in a department store. His adolescent daughter dates an auto mechanic's son; he's satisfied, since he is "a good Christian boy," by which he means a churchgoing Baptist. He has another adolescent girl and a boy who is in grade school.

But Mr. Gardner is a haunted man. He worries obsessively that he will have a heart attack or some other abruptly fatal illness. He dreads death. He endlessly debates with himself whether he should sell his property and "take it easy" in order to avoid the business stresses that he fears will kill him; however, he cannot sit quietly for more than fifteen minutes and would find retirement unbearable. He is the treasurer of his church congregation, and during services he tallies up the collection in a back room because he cannot sit through a service; he becomes too restless. He gets taut, even panicky, if he must sit for more than several minutes in a noisy, crowded room.

He has anxiety attacks once or twice a month; waves of severe apprehension pass over him. His pulse pounds rapidly, his breath comes in shallow pants, and he is convinced that he is about to die. These episodes last from ten minutes to an hour or more. On numerous occasions his wife has driven him to the Clay County Memorial Hospital during anxiety spells; there the intern or his family doctor listens to his heart, takes his blood pressure, tells him it's "just nerves," and gives him a sedative. Mr. Gardner has been coming to see me twice a week for two months. He works fairly well in psychotherapy.

He begins to talk. He has made a few notes, which he lays on the small table beside his chair.

"I've been thinking a lot about our last session, Doctor.

194

About the death of my mother. To tell the truth, I really can't remember much about it. Over the weekend I talked with my brother about her. He doesn't remember much either; he's younger than I am. But he told me a few things, and they jogged a few more things inside me.

"My mother was always a sick woman. At least, that's the way I remember her. I think there was something wrong with her chest. She coughed a lot. It seems I mainly remember her lying in bed. In fact, right at this minute, I can't clearly remember seeing her out of bed very much, though I must have. She didn't die until I was twelve. She had us two children, my brother and me. But all I can remember is her lying in bed, by the window, looking out. And it always seems to have been a dark day. Always rain or snow or cloudy. And her propped up on pillows and coughing.

"And my father would tell us to be quiet and not to make noise because my mother was sick. The house was very quiet. It was on East Twenty-eighth Street, a large old house, and her room was on the second floor facing the street. Twenty-eighth Street was a quiet street then, with lots of big, old elm trees. It's all been torn down to put the freeway in.

"But then, when I think of my mother, I also see her as being angry at us kids a lot of the time. My father said not to pay any attention, that she was sick and nervous. But he wasn't home much. He worked long hours. He was gone in the morning before we got up. We made our own breakfast and went to school. Sometimes a colored girl came in to help my mother. I guess she got Mother's meals for her. The girls never lasted long. A couple of months or so. My mother yelled at them and pretty soon they left. She said they all stole. Maybe some of them did. I don't know.

"It was always dark when my father got home. He would go up to see my mother. Then he would come down and get his dinner and read the paper. Sometimes he listened to the radio, but not much. He worked six days a week. He was a checker at the stockyards. I never was sure just what a checker did; I still don't know. My father was a very silent man; he never talked much. Sundays he took us to church and in the afternoon he puttered around the house. I remember him and mother sometimes sitting on the swing on the front porch when she was stronger. But I don't remember that very clearly."

There are contradictions, repetitions, and some implausible things in Mr. Gardner's talk. There always are in psychotherapy. The patient is exploring, poking into painful areas and withdrawing, and then going back. The accuracy of his recollections, moreover, is often of secondary importance; what he thinks happened and how he felt about it are frequently more significant than what actually did happen.

He paused and leaned forward. "One day—I didn't remember this until my brother mentioned something about it—my mother was in the kitchen. She was always thin. A tall, thin woman. I came running in from the yard. She screamed at me, 'Look at you. You're tracking mud all over the linoleum, and I just got through mopping it up.' She yelled that I was causing her sicknesses, that I was putting gray hairs in her head, and that I ruined everything she did. My brother ran in and then she started yelling at both of us. She said that we were both driving her to an early grave, that she would have a nervous breakdown, that she would die, and that we'd feel sorry then for what we'd done to her. She threw a pan at my brother, but he ducked and it hit the wall. I guess that's why he remembered that day so well and why I now remember it so clearly. Because of the pan. It made a mark in the plaster where it hit, and the mark was there for a long time. Maybe years.

"We just stood there. 'Get out, get out,' she yelled, and we ran out into the backyard again. It started to rain, and we stayed in the garage until it was dark and Dad came home. I think she talked to us like that lots of times. In fact, many, many times. I seem to remember her standing on the back porch steps screaming at us, and the neighbors looking out of their windows and from their backyards to see what was going on. That happened mainly when it was hot, but I think I remember it also happening when there weren't any leaves on the trees and it was cold. Yes, it must have happened a lot of times, one way or another."

"You must have felt very guilty and frightened when she talked like that," I say.

"I guess so. I feel sort of upset now when I talk about it. Did I tell you about her nervous breakdown?"

"No, you have not told me about that. You have not mentioned it at all."

"I thought I did. I felt sure I did."

"Perhaps it means something that you haven't been able to mention it until now."

"Maybe. It must have been when I was nine or ten. I remember that I was still wearing knickers. We wore knickers that went down to below our knees and woolen stockings covering our legs in the winter. In the summer we wore short pants. I didn't wear long trousers until I was eleven and a half, when I began to get taller.

"Anyway, my mother was in the psychiatric hospital at Coatsville. It's an osteopathic psychiatric hospital. My father took me to see her one weekend. Why he took me I don't know. Maybe he thought it would be good for her. Maybe she asked to see me. We went by train.

"When we got to the hospital, we went up a long flight of stairs and the attendant looked at us through a little barred window in a heavy metal door. My father said, 'I'm Mr. Gardner. I've come to see my wife.' They opened the door and we went in.

197

"There were some people sitting on wooden benches along the wall in a large, bare room. One or two of them were talking loudly to nobody in particular, but the rest just sat and stared or looked around. A woman in a white uniform went over to a bench, and then I saw my mother. She looked awful. She was thinner than usual, and her hair hung down; I guess nobody combed it and put hairpins in it.

"'It's your husband and your boy come to see you, Mrs. Gardner,' the woman said, but my mother didn't move.

"The woman told her to get up. Then she took my mother by the arm and we all went down the hall to her room. The woman sat my mother down on a low bed with an iron rail head and foot, and we sat down on another bed opposite it.

"The nurse, or attendant, said for us to have a nice chat, and she walked out.

"My father said, 'Sarah, how are you?'

"My mother stared at me and then looked at him. 'I want to go home,' she said.

"My father said she could go home as soon as she was well.

"She repeated that she wanted to go home right then.

"My father said that she could go home when the doctors felt she was able to, but that she was still a nervous, sick woman. He said it was up to the doctors.

"She started to cry and rubbed her hands together and talked about a lot of things I couldn't understand. I think it was pretty mixed up.

"My father began to get very upset. He turned on me and said, 'Look what you and your brother have driven your mother to. Are you satisfied now?'

"It went on and on, with her sobbing like that and him talking first to her and then to me. He was half trying to reason with her and half blaming it all on me. Finally it was over. We left. As we went out of the building, I remember one man sticking his skinny arms out a barred window and shouting at us. We walked to the railroad station, caught the evening train, and came home.

"It's strange that I should remember all those things so strongly right now. However, I think that's the way it was. Anyway, that is what comes into my mind as I think about it. I'm sure I couldn't imagine all this. It must have happened, but it seems like a bad dream. My brother doesn't remember anything about this, but he was younger and I don't think he ever went to see her in the hospital. All the same, I think it must have been more or less like that."

"That was a very painful experience for a boy of nine or ten. It must have left you feeling very guilty," I say.

For a couple of minutes he looks silently at his clenched hands, over which he is hunched. There are moments in psychotherapy when two minutes, two hours, and twenty years are all the same thing. His face is a grimace. The frightened boy, the troubled adolescent, and the panicky businessman are lost in one blur of pain.

"Sometimes," I say, "a child who goes through an experience like that feels that he has a heavy debt to pay. He feels that he perhaps must suffer something like that which he inflicted on others."

We sit in silence for another minute while he sucks his lower lip between his teeth.

I go on. "This happened at a sensitive time in your life. It is quite possible that for a long time, months or years, you felt that, at least in part, you caused both the physical and mental illnesses of your mother. Later you perhaps were tormented by fears that you caused her death."

I pause. He sits motionless looking at his fists, which are resting on his knees. It is impossible to know what my words mean to him just now or even whether he is listening to them.

I proceed: "These are very painful things to think about

and talk about. Perhaps that is why it has taken you two months to speak about them here with me."

This is a lot for him to digest, far too much, in fact. We undoubtedly shall return to this area of his life many times, from many points of view, in the coming months.

He stops chewing his lip. "I remember that in church, when the time came for the preacher to say that we should all silently ask forgiveness for our sins, I used to ask God to forgive me for any sickness I ever caused anyone. But I don't know whether that was when I was a boy or a teenager or maybe even later. I remember, too, that I had a sort of superstitious feeling that if I didn't say the words 'Forgive us the trouble we have caused unto others' many times every day that I might die before sundown. I must have had that feeling a long time, but I don't connect it with my mother."

He pauses for a minute, visibly straining to remember. "I had that feeling until a short time before I got married. Not that getting married had anything to do with its going away. But I remember that I didn't feel that way and have to say those words anymore after I got married."

He sits back in his chair and looks at me. The wrinkles are gone from his face, and he appears tired.

Silence.

"Your mother must have recovered from her mental illness," I say, "for she died at home, you told me. I assume she was mentally all right at the time of her death." This last was half a statement and half a question.

"Yes, yes," he says, narrowing his eyes slightly and working it out slowly. "But I don't remember her coming home, or at least I don't remember it right now. However, I was twelve when she died, and she was only in the mental hospital a few months. I can't fit it all together. There are just pieces here and there, and it's hard to know which comes after which and what goes where."

"Painful things from childhood and early adolescence have a way of being poked back out of awareness," I say. "But they don't go away. They smoulder on, and perhaps much later in life they produce fearfulness, panicky spells, or persistent worries."

I do not expect Mr. Gardner to assimilate much of this now. We are simply sketching the dim outlines of a picture that we shall spend many months filling in.

He picks up his small sheet of notes from the side table, tears the paper into small squares, and puts them neatly into the ashtray.

"When I was a kid I used to have nightmares," he says. "I think I had a lot of them. I can remember my father and brother waking up lots of times and telling me to stop shouting."

He stops and glances about the room a little anxiously. The light is fading behind the Venetian blinds as it grows dim outside. I flick a wall switch behind me that turns on a bright lamp on a small table in a corner behind him. This clears the darkness that has been gradually increasing.

"Tell me what you remember about your nightmares," I say.

"I only remember one of them clearly, right now," he replies. "But I am sure that I had that one many times. It was a weird one. When you think about it, it wasn't particularly frightening, but I sometimes woke up screaming after it. It's been forty years, maybe more, since I last had it.

"I would dream that I was in a large room. The room was enormous. It was like an endless hotel lobby or the old waiting room at the Union Station. There were large numbers of people sitting around in groups, on benches, chairs, and sofas. They had different kinds of clothing. Some were dressed in white robes, like the Romans in history books. Others were dressed like people of one hundred years ago or as in the time of George Washington. Some had on strange clothing, like people in the Middle Ages. There were men, women, and children. The air was filled with that kind of low noise there always is in a big lobby or a bus station or a railroad station. The room was sort of dim, but you could still see everything.

"Every once in a while a man would come to the top of the stairs. I forgot to mention the stairs. At one side of the room was a huge stairs, very wide and very long. It was made of white stone, maybe marble, and had stone banisters at each side. It went up to what seemed like another place, where it was lighter. I felt that it was like another world. Anyway, every once in a while a man would come to the top of the stairs with a long roll of paper, and he would begin to read off names. When he started, everybody became still; the noise stopped. As he read the names, a few people here and there got up and began to go up the stairs, and others began to cry. The people going up the stairs never looked back. And the man with the long roll of paper went away.

"Then everything went back to what it had been, and the noise started up again. Finally I turned to the man next to me and asked him something. I don't know what it was. But he looked at me and said, 'Your time hasn't come yet. We're still in the third century B.C.' Then I would wake up, very scared, sometimes crying and yelling. My father or my brother would tell me to calm down.

"That's the only dream I can remember right now from my childhood. I remember that there was another dream about a man with a long, pointed nose who was in the Dick Tracy comic strip at that time, but I can't remember any of the details."

When he started to tell me about his dream, I picked up his chart from my desk, leafed through it to the current page, and made careful notes about it. I also made about twenty lines of notes on other things he had talked about and added some of the things I had said.

I glance at the clock on the table behind him. It is about ten minutes before six.

"Mr. Gardner, we don't have time to attempt to explore your dream today. We shall go into it another time. However, it seems to be the dream of a fearful boy who dreaded what the future had in store for him. That is perhaps its most superficial level. Other things are hidden beneath the surface of the dream, and perhaps we can dissect them out in time.

"I think it is clear to both of us that you have talked about some important things today, things that give us clues about what happened in your childhood to lay the foundations of the anxiety spells, fears of illness, and other emotional distresses that plague you now."

After a brief pause I give him a short summary: "If you think about it, the things we have talked about today in relation to your mother are the things you dread in yourself—physical diseases, severe mental illness, and death. Of course, there is no more chance that any of these things will happen to you than they will happen to me or anyone out on the street. But I think we are beginning to discover some of the old wounds that have festered in you for a long time and that probably are closely related to the discomforts that bring you to see me."

In psychotherapy there rarely are abrupt revelations and dramatic moments of self-understanding. Insight is achieved by tedious, repetitive examinations of significant areas of the patient's life. The same relationships, events, and feelings are approached many times from various points of view. Psychotherapy also may be likened to the gradual emergence of an old painting by the meticulous, patient, bit-by-bit removal of layers of obscuring dirt; it is not like the abrupt unveiling of a clear picture.

203

He sits back in the chair, his hands resting on its two cushioned arm ends.

These two arm ends, incidentally, become so soiled with the grease and sweat of patients' palms that they must be reupholstered once or twice a year.

"I think we must stop now and go on next time, Mr. Gardner. I'll put you down for Friday at five, as usual. The receptionist has left. You can let yourself out."

We part.

I gather together from a back corner of my desk the charts of the patients I have seen this afternoon and place them in a drawer of my desk. Marie has keys to my desk and my filing cabinets and will put the charts away in the morning. I then lock my desk and also lock the filing cabinets in an adjoining large closet. I check the spindle on Marie's neat, glass-topped desk in the waiting room. There is a two-line typewritten note, reminding me of the places and times of my two hospital meetings tonight. I crumple the paper and toss it into the wastebasket.

I turn out the lights and leave the office, twisting the doorknob a couple of times and rattling the door slightly to make sure it is locked. There have been a few robberies in doctors' offices in our building during the past few months.

I go down the empty corridor, out onto the wide veranda that runs along the front and sides of the office building, and down the lighted steps to the parking lot. The light snow that fell during the morning squeaks under my feet as I cross the cement parking lot. It is dark now.

I am not tired, but I will be in another couple of hours; I am used to the life I lead.

I get into my car. The main rush-hour traffic is over in our section of the city, and I head for St. Catharine's.

12

6:10. I arrived in the doctors' dining room at St. Catharine's, where a dozen psychiatrists were sitting at a long table eating overboiled chicken à la king. The departmental meeting would begin shortly.

A word of explanation about hospital departmental and staff meetings is perhaps necessary. Once every two or three months, depending on the particular hospital's rules, each hospital has an evening general staff meeting for all physicians on the staff; this may include from one hundred to four hundred doctors. In addition, each specialty (pediatrics, surgery, psychiatry, and others) has a departmental meeting once each month. These meetings usually are held in the early evening and combine a dinner with the business to be done. In order to maintain his privileges of admitting patients to the hospital, each physician must attend 75 percent of these meetings or be excused from them in writing for legitimate reasons. Without this requirement the meetings would be sparsely attended.

The purpose of these meetings is to discuss any plans and problems of the department or the general medical staff. The governing boards of most hospitals are composed of prominent business men, lawyers, and civic-minded women, and many matters of purely medical nature are left in the hands of the general medical staff or the particular specialty department involved. The various specialty departments and the general medical staff also may pass resolutions urging the board of directors or the hospital's administrators to do or not to do a wide range of things. The board of directors and the administrators usually give careful attention to whatever the physicians recommend, but sometimes there are conflicting points of view that must be settled in committee meetings.

In Catholic hospitals there may be two boards, a lay board of interested community leaders and another board composed of sisters of the particular religious order that owns the hospital and is responsible for it. The sisters usually defer to the opinions of the lay board and the physicians' committees on important decisions. The general tendency in recent years has been to put more responsibility and control of Catholic hospitals in the hands of civic-minded Catholic laymen, but the religious order usually is also represented. This trend has to a large extent been caused by the sharply decreasing number of sisters in many religious orders.

Departmental and staff meetings vary much in nature from one hospital to the next and from one meeting to another, depending on the physicians' personalities and how interested or lethargic they are about the hospital's activities. Each department and each general staff has a chairman, a vice chairman, and a secretary. Minutes of each meeting are kept and are entered in a special section of the hospital's central record room or the adminstrator's office. Hospital accreditation commissions (which certify the fitness of hospitals) require that these minutes are properly recorded and kept.

The departmental and staff meetings at Mt. Sinai usually are long, argumentative, and boring. The meetings at St. Catharine's are brief and orderly unless there is some issue of special interest to be decided. The departmental meetings at Bethesda Hospital are rubber-stamp formalities that are raced through with disgraceful speed; half the doctors arrive and sign the attendance sheet after the meeting has ended. The meetings at Elmdale Hospital are desultory social occasions with good roast beef and free beer to all.

I sit down at St. Catharine's. Greetings are exchanged around the table, and I dig into chicken à la king and boiled vegetables that a girl brings from the adjacent hospital kitchen. I glance down the table at the assembled psychiatrists.

The Infernal Quartet are there, a pestilent foursome. Dr. Arthur Downs is senior man of this four-man psychiatric group, which occupies a large suite of offices in a suburban office building. He was reared shabbily by an alcoholic father and a mother who came from the shoddy fringes of genteel society and an old Kansas City family. Arthur had polio as a child; one leg is half an inch shorter than the other, and he limps when he walks. He has been struggling all his life to make it, both professionally and socially, and he has. He knows a wide section of the social elite in Kansas City, plays poker with prominent businessmen, and knows six hundred physicians by their first names; for every doctor he has a broad smile and a friendly inquiry.

To Arthur, patients are cattle with checkbooks, and he has lucrative ways of handling them. Everyone who looks sad is diagnosed "psychotic depression" and is given electroshock therapy three times a week at the highest going rate for such treatment on the Kansas City market. Silent people who act a little odd are termed "schizophrenic," and they too are given electroshock treatment. Talkative patients who are restless are called "manic," and electricity is prescribed for them too. Most neurotics (as well as the occasional true psychotics who drift into Arthur's hands) can be cast into one of these three diagnostic categories. Those who cannot be jammed into one of these classifications are told that they need psychotherapy, and for this Arthur has a bumbling, middle-aged social worker on his staff. Her incompetence soon drives away these unprofitable items (the cost of a three-minute electroshock treatment and a fifty-minute psychotherapeutic hour are the same in Kansas City); she sees them for fifteen- or twenty-minute sessions. If the "psychotherapy" patients drop out and complain to their family physicians about the way they were handled, Arthur explains that the patient "didn't cooperate in treatment." Since many general physicians find neurotic patients puzzling and annoying, they usually accept his explanation.

The economic basis (and what other basis is there?) for this setup is electroshock treatment. If the energy crisis were to become desperate and the Kansas City Power and Light Company collapsed, Arthur Downs and his three partners would be smashed. The Infernal Quartet always have at least fifty to sixty patients scattered throughout the various psychiatric wards in town; at times the number runs significantly higher than that. I estimate the gross income of this four-man group at more than a million dollars a year. Of course, Uncle Sam takes a big bite of that, but there's still plenty left for Arthur and his associates.

Why does Arthur need three colleagues, and who are they? Wouldn't it be simpler just to hire a couple of young assistants on salary and pocket almost all the loot himself? No. I'll explain.

Dr. Larry Packard, nominally the number two member of the group, is an anxious, insecure man; however, despite his problems, he is well liked in the medical community of Kansas City and thus increases the number of referring physicians who funnel patients into the group. Larry is almost an alcoholic; he is a weak man and Arthur dominates him utterly. Nonetheless, I suspect that Larry has a conscience and the way he practices psychiatry probably bothers him at times, but between sedation by alcohol and bullying by Arthur, his conscience is kept under control.

They still need two more men. The sheer amount of physical running around, paperwork, committee-meeting attendance, and public-relations contacts demands it. Thus, when the practice got big enough about ten years ago, Arthur brought in Bryan Redford. Bryan is the public-relations man of the group. He is a charming, witty speaker, and he tirelessly holds forth on psychiatric subjects at women's groups, businessmen's luncheons, parent-teacher association meetings, rural medical society meetings, and various other types of gatherings.

How does Bryan get invited to address all these meetings? It's really quite simple. He is on the speakers committees of both the Jackson County Medical Society (Kansas City, Missouri) and the Wyandotte County Medical Society (Kansas City, Kansas), and he snaps up all requests that come in for psychiatric speakers. Also, over the years he has acquired the reputation of being an ever-available, entertaining speaker on any kind of psychiatric topic, and many requests now come directly to him. Most of what he says is rubbish, but it is amusing rubbish. I suspect that a good deal of his material is ghostwritten in Chicago or St. Louis (it's a tax-deductible professional expense, and so it costs the Infernal Quartet only thirty-five to forty cents on the dollar). However, Bryan may concoct his own speeches; he is a clever conversationalist and may dream many of them up himself. He certainly enjoys delivering them and fielding the questions afterward with a rapid stream of witticisms and epigrams; I've seen him in action a couple of times.

The fourth member of the Infernal Quartet is Ramsey Burns. He is young, not too bright, and enjoys making two or three times more money than he anticipated. Arthur controls him by charm and money, and Ramsey is content to coast along in the comfortable berth he has found. He does much of the running from hospital to hospital to push buttons on electroshock machines. Moreover, this group is a legal partnership, with shares running from Arthur's 40 percent to Ramsey's 10 percent. Ramsey is twenty years younger than his three colleagues, and when his seniors retire to nursing homes or ascend to receive their well-earned rewards, this mint gradually will fall into his hands. I think he's already thought of this.

Why doesn't the medical society or somebody do something about the Infernal Quartet? There are various reasons. Doctors are notoriously unwilling to police their own ranks. Such policing involves infringements on their traditional liberty and independence, and in addition there is the tricky question about who would do the policing. If committees were set up by the medical society or by hospital staffs to supervise professional practices, it is probable that one or more members of the Infernal Quartet would end up on each committee devoted to psychiatry. Moreover, since only a physician has the technical skill to evaluate another physician, laymen could not do the job. In psychiatry this problem is made immensely more difficult by the very different opinions that various schools of psychiatric thought have about almost all methods of treatment.

There are other factors that contribute to the prosperity and safety of the Infernal Quartet. They may be horrible psychiatrists, but they are superb politicians. Through endless entertaining of physicians and their wives at dinners, brunches, cocktail parties, theater parties, and other occasions, they keep their medico-political fences well mended. Referring doctors feel that they are "regular fellows," "down-to-earth, practical psychiatrists," and "not

210

up in the clouds all the time like so many psychiatrists are."
In some cases, of course, after a few years a perceptive
doctor may begin to wonder why everybody he refers to
them gets electroshock treatment. However, if a referring
physician makes only three or four psychiatric referrals a
year, and if some of his referrals genuinely need electroshock, and if a few others somehow escape it, it may take
many years before he begins to understand what is going
on.

The Infernal Quartet are in constant social and professional circulation with about twelve hundred doctors over a
ten-county area, and although they have many acquaint-
ances, no one really knows them well. Also, they are out of
town a significant amount of time. Each of them takes a
three- or four-week vacation, often abroad, twice a year, in
addition to brief trips to state and national medical
conventions. Thus, for nine months during the year only
three of them are in town, and for about two months in the
year only two of them are in Kansas City. The system is so
well set up that with the aid of efficient secretaries and
nurse assistants, two men can run it as well as three or four
for brief periods of time. During the six weeks between
Thanksgiving and New Year's Day, when the medical
entertainment circuit of cocktail parties and dinners is in
full swing, all four of them are in town, and they do more
than their share of the entertaining.

The Infernal Quartet are the only real devils at the St.
Catharine's departmental meeting tonight. Ted Peters, Bill
Straus, five other psychiatrists, and myself make up
tonight's even dozen at the table. Most of them are decent,
well-trained fellows.

As the chicken and mashed potatoes disappear and the
ice cream and coffee come, the meeting begins. Roy Havens
is departmental chairman this year. While half the doctors
are still eating their ice cream, he calls the meeting to order.

Frank Mulvaney, the secretary, reads the minutes of the last meeting. They are approved without corrections or additions. The chairman inquires if there is any old business. Dishes are being cleared away, and cigarettes and cigars are lighted.

There are two items of old business. A letter from Sister Elaine Elliot, the hospital's assistant administrator, is read, reporting that a new occupational therapist for the psychiatric ward has been hired to replace Mrs. Terman, who left when her husband was transferred to Denver recently. Also, there is a memorandum from Mr. Conway, the hospital's attorney; it is countersigned by Sister Elaine Elliot. It states that all patients who come to the emergency room after making suicidal attempts must have psychiatric evaluation before discharge from the emergency room unless they and their relatives refuse it. This merely makes an existing practice official; it is being written into the hospital's procedure book as a protection against lawsuits. Almost all patients seen in the emergency room after suicidal attempts are hospitalized for at least several days of study on the psychiatric ward at St. Catharine's or elsewhere. Patients who refuse this recommendation are asked to sign a form to that effect, and if they refuse to sign the form, the nurse and intern or other attending physician on duty sign the form with a notation that the patient refused to do so.

The chairman asks if there is any new business. Ted Peters has a piece of new business. He makes a motion that the existing admission policy of first-come-first-served on the psychiatric ward be changed to one in which all the doctors on the staff have an equal number of allotted beds, and that any doctor's quota can be infringed only if he does not fill it, and that when a doctor has less than his quota of patients on the ward any new patient whom he wishes to admit shall have preference over the patients of physicians whose quotas are full. Bill Straus seconds the motion. The chairman has the secretary read the motion, states that it has been made and seconded, and declares the subject open for discussion.

The explosion begins.

Why is there an explosion over such a reasonable-sounding proposal? It occurs because this motion stabs at the heart of an important medico-economic problem.

Under the existing admission system at St. Catharine's a psychiatrist who has a patient to admit to the psychiatric ward calls the admission office. If a bed is available, his patient is admitted at once. If not, he can seek a bed at any other psychiatric facility where he has admitting privileges, or he can put the patient on the waiting list for a bed at St. Catharine's. If there are from one to three patients on the waiting list at St. Catharine's, he probably puts his patient on the waiting list, since at the usual daily discharge rate from the ward, he is almost sure to get his patient in within a day or two. If there are several or more patients on the waiting list, the delay as a rule will be from several to ten days or so. In about 80 percent of cases most of the physicians cannot hold a patient needing hospitalization that long.

However, though this present system may sound sensible and fair, its practical result is that the patients of the Infernal Quartet continually occupy at least 60 to 70 percent of the psychiatric beds. When the ward is full, as it often is, the Infernal Quartet pile up their neurotic patients, whom they have classified as schizophrenics or depressives, on the waiting list. Thus, the other dozen psychiatrists on the staff, who classify and treat patients as they should be classified and treated, often find their patients at the end of a waiting list that may run from twelve to fifteen

213

patients. The neurotic patients of the Infernal Quartet can wait; they're not very disturbed and nothing urgent need be done about them.

However, a strongly suicidal patient or a highly agitated schizophrenic of one of the other psychiatrists on the staff of St. Catharine's cannot wait. The urgent patient must be hospitalized somewhere within forty-eight to seventy-two hours. Hence, he is not put on the waiting list at St. Catharine's; he is sent to some other psychiatric service in town. After this system has been going for thirty days, the Infernal Quartet's patients occupy 70 percent or occasionally more of the beds at St. Catharine's.

Nobody except Arthur Downs and his partners likes the existing system. The other psychiatrists, the sisters, the psychiatric nurses and aides, and all others who understand what is going on detest the Infernal Quartet. However, since Arthur and his three associates control four votes in the department, and often there are only five or six doctors at the departmental meetings, and since physicians as a rule hesitate to disturb relationships with each other, this arrangement has dragged on for years. However, during the last year three new psychiatrists have joined the staff at St. Catharine's, and the percentage of votes controlled by the Quartet in the department has decreased.

Doctors tend not to rock each other's boats until conditions become unbearable; they have become unbearable at St. Catharine's, and some boat rocking is about to begin. If this motion receives a majority of votes at this meeting, it will go into effect at once, since each department may determine its own admission policies.

If this motion is passed, the admission procedure will be as follows: If Dr. Peters (or any physician except one of the Infernal Quartet) calls the admission office for a bed, and if there is a waiting list, and if Dr. Peters has less than his quota of beds filled, Dr. Peters' patient will go to the head of the waiting list and his patient will be admitted within a day or two. Similarly, every physician except the Quartet (who can always be counted on to have their quota filled) will get his patients admitted preferentially until all physicians have roughly the same number of patients in the hospital. Thus, the percentage of beds occupied by patients of the Quartet, especially during the times of the year when beds are scarce, will fall from 70 percent to about 25 percent, which is their percentage of the total number of psychiatrists at St. Catharine's.

Twelve doctors are present tonight; four are absent. This is a high attendance rate. Ted Peters has chosen a good time to bring up his motion. He probably has been waiting several months for this opportunity. The Infernal Quartet are all there, though they are in a minority; if the motion passes, they will have no grounds for remonstrance, and it will be permanent.

However, it is still doubtful that the motion will pass. To defeat it, the Quartet will have to get only two other votes in addition to their own. They very possibly can do so. Old Dr. Morgan, who admits few patients and is a long-term friend of Arthur Downs, may well vote with them. Sid Cummings, who does more neurology than psychiatry and does all the electroencephalograms and neurological consultations for the Quartet also may vote with them. Another physician or two, convinced that the motion will fail and seeing no point in alienating Arthur Downs and his colleagues, also may vote against it or abstain. In addition, under the hospital's rules the motion does not pass with a six-six vote. (In small meetings of this kind the chairman votes on all issues.)

This is medical infighting at its best, an exhilarating spectacle when one understands the issues and personalities involved. A great deal of money is at stake. However, much more depends on this vote. If the motion passes, the psychiatric ward at St. Catharine's can cease to be an electroshock parlor and can become more what a psychiatric ward should be, with better activity programs and a more therapeutic atmosphere.

The discussion takes fifteen minutes. Tempers rise. Ted Peters and Bill Straus speak out strongly in favor of the motion, stressing the fairness of equal beds for each doctor and citing the policies of two other psychiatric wards in town. Arthur Downs says the proposed system would cause chaos, and Larry Packard echoes him. Dr. Morgan says that since the measure apparently is so controversial, perhaps we ought to think about it until the next meeting. I say that I favor it because it will cut down the hospital's monthly electricity bill. Nobody laughs, and Arthur Downs glares at me angrily. I smile blandly at him and annoy him further by mentioning that I recently read a particularly worrying article on the energy crisis. In my elfin way I have hit at the central problem, which no one else defines. The other doctors are silent, but nobody is bored at this meeting.

Bryan Redford makes a motion to table the motion. Arthur Downs seconds it. The vote is six-six; it does not pass, and so Ted Peters' motion is still on the agenda. I assume that Arthur Downs will win again tonight, as usual, since it appears that his opposition cannot muster the seven votes they need to pass Ted's motion. After two minutes of more discussion Arthur Downs moves that a committee be appointed to discuss the matter with the administration and the admission office before a final vote is taken. It is seconded by Ramsey Burns and is voted down seven to five. Someone calls for the question. Bryan Redford launches into one of his witty monologues, but is interrupted by increasingly insistent calls for the question. These doctors haven't seen their families since early this morning.

Bryan gives up, the chairman asks the secretary to read the motion again, and takes the vote. All in favor are asked to raise their right hands, and all opposed are thereafter asked to signify similarly. The motion is carried eight to four. Dr. Morgan put principle ahead of his friendship for Arthur Downs, and Sid Cummings will get no more requests for electroencephalograms and neurological consultations from the Infernal Quartet. This will cost Sid Cummings several thousand dollars a year, and he knows it. I am surprised that the motion passed and even more surprised by the size of the majority. At moments like this I am glad that I'm a doctor and have hopes about where we are going. There are other times when I cannot indulge in the luxury of this feeling.

The chairman asks if there is any other new business. There is none. Is there a motion to adjourn? Yes. It is made, seconded, and carried. The meeting is over.

Arthur Downs walks out rapidly and Larry Packard runs after him. Bryan Redford and Ramsey Burns go out with a couple of others.

Ted Peters and I leave together. Our cars are parked side by side in the doctors' parking lot.

"Arthur was furious," Ted says. "They've been cut down to size here at St. Catharine's."

"Sister Mary Lawrence will be delighted," I say. "Within a month or so she'll have one-third or one-fourth as much electroshock on her ward, and she will be able to get a good activity program going. Also, she won't be ashamed to show the place to her student nurses."

"Larry Packard was scared shitless. He'll probably go home and get drunk. Arthur will be mad for three days," Ted says.

"Don't worry about them," I say. "They'll find more beds elsewhere. That crew can take care of themselves."

"I'm not worried about them," Ted says. "I'm just glad we've put them in their place here at St. Catharine's."

We get into our cars and leave.

13

I glanced at my watch as I parked my car in front of Elmdale Hospital. 7:15. I went in, took the elevator to the second floor, and went into a large dining room. About forty psychiatrists and others had just finished dinner, and a monthly staff meeting was beginning. Half a dozen stragglers from the St. Catharine's meeting came in shortly after I did. Herb Monroe, the hospital director and psychiatrist in chief, came over and greeted each of us, offering beer and a buffet supper to anyone who wanted them. He acted and looked like the genial proprietor of a neighborhood bar. Elmdale Hospital is never sufficiently heated, and Herb wore a smart woolen sweater under his suit coat.

About 60 percent of the psychiatrists in Kansas City were there. Dr. Foster, a short, balding man, was reading the minutes of the last meeting. Any corrections or amendments? Dr. Bohrman, who practices in Kansas City, Kansas, got up and said that the discussion of the proposed change in visiting hours had been left out. Thank you, Dr. Bohrman. That addition would be made. Any other corrections or amendments? No. The minutes of the last meeting stood approved.

Is there any old business? Lord, yes! There always is at Elmdale Hospital.

218

Letters have been sent to Blue Cross and Blue Shield on the new contract being negotiated with them. In the hospital's letter of February 17 it was proposed that. . . .

I am not listening. I am looking for the attendance sheet. At last I see it. It is passing from table to table and from hand to hand, as one doctor after another signs it and thus gets a credit toward the 75 percent of such meetings that he must attend each year to maintain the privilege of admitting patients to Elmdale. I see the general direction the sheet is taking. At a strategic point I rise and go to the table where it is. I nod, whisper greetings to the doctors at the table, reach over, and scribble my name on the paper. I then retreat to my table. My entire purpose in coming to this meeting has been accomplished. I now can slip out at any convenient moment and go home.

Elmdale Hospital and the Monroe family who control it are hardy weeds in the psychiatric garden. Until the late 1940's private psychiatric sanatoriums (as they were called) were profit-making enterprises, and there were about ten of them, with between fifteen and sixty beds each, in Kansas City. Their proprietors were physicians with varying degrees of psychiatric training, and they ran their hospitals with the aid of two or three physician assistants. Until the late 1940's, with the exception of a dungeon in the corner of the Kansas City General Hospital, these proprietory hospitals were the only psychiatric facilities in the Kansas City area.

During the boom in hospital construction with the aid of federal-government funds after the Second World War, all these profit-making private hospitals, with the exception of Elmdale, went out of business. As Mt. Sinai, St. Catharine's, and half a dozen other Kansas City hospitals built psychiatric divisions, and the General Hospital and the medical schools built good psychiatric sections, the flow of patients to the private sanatoriums slowed to a trickle and then stopped. Their physician-proprietors retired, often selling their hospitals and adjoining grounds to real estate developers. A couple of these hospitals were refurbished and reopened in the 1960's and 1970's as nursing homes for the ever-increasing number of senile persons whose families could not manage them at home.

Only Elmdale has survived. It has survived because of a variety of factors. Herb Monroe, the third generation of the Monroe family to run this hospital since it was opened by his grandfather about 1905, is a shrewd businessman and an able politician. He doesn't know much about psychiatry, but he knows how to handle people and money. He also is very good at knowing which way the wind is blowing.

Elmdale Hospital occupies a huge, high-ceilinged old building that was a county general hospital for the first three decades of this century. The county ran short of money in 1931, closed the hospital, and sold the building to the Monroe family; until that time the Monroes had been operating in a much smaller building, converted from a mansion, on the edge of town. They probably got the building cheaply since they had good connections with the Pendergast political machine, which dominated Kansas City at that time. The fact that Herb's father, who then ran the hospital, knew a minor Pendergast politician named Harry S. Truman possibly facilitated the deal. My father also had dealings with Mr. Truman. During the late 1920's my father ran a laundry chain in Kansas City, and as one of the conditions for getting the laundry business of the McCune Home for Boys and other county institutions, Mr. Truman insisted that my father's company do the Truman family's laundry free each week for several years. In about 1930 my father quit the laundry business and did his last favor for Harry Truman. A scant fifteen years later Mr.

220

Truman became President of the United States and the most powerful man in the world. It was he who made the decision to drop the two atom bombs that killed 150,000 people.

The Elmdale Hospital has one sterling virtue; it always has a bed. When every other psychiatric service in town is full, and a psychiatrist has on his hands a schizophrenic who just threatened the neighbors with a loaded rifle or a depressed patient who just tried to poison himself, and hospitalization cannot be delayed, Elmdale has a bed. If the patient has hospitalization insurance, or if his family has a five-hundred-dollar down payment, in he goes. The psychiatrist can treat the patient there or can transfer him to another hospital when a bed becomes available elsewhere.

Elmdale is gruesome, with its slatternly practical nurses, unshaven aides, dirty board floors, and rusty bars on the windows. However, it has served me in many crises and doubtless will continue to do so in the future. I use it as a way station on the road to something better for very sick patients. Two or three elderly Kansas City psychiatrists take all their patients there, and Elmdale has a staff of three full-time psychiatrists in addition to Herb. Most of the patients referred directly to the full-time staff of Elmdale come from middle-aged and elderly family physicians practicing in small towns and rural areas in Western Missouri and Eastern Kansas; it is the only psychiatric facility they know in Kansas City, and Herb Monroe makes sure that minor Christmas presents and courteous reports about their patients maintain these contacts.

The only one of Elmdale's full-time staff members for whom most Kansas City psychiatrists have any respect is Eugen Singer, an elderly widower who came there as a refugee from Hitler's Germany in the 1930's. He lives with a spinster sister in a small cottage on the hospital grounds.

He still practices psychiatry more or less as he knew it in Germany in the 1930's, but he does it conscientiously and humanely. Besides a little electroshock therapy and a few antipsychotic medications, he has added nothing to his repertoire of treatments and ideas that he learned as a young man in Munich in the hospital where the great Kraepelin was once psychiatrist in chief.

The other two full-time psychiatrists at Elmdale are flotsam who have drifted into this safe, quiet professional bay where they are protected from the turbulent waters of independent practice. One is Dr. Franklin, a fifty-five-year-old, thin, smiling man in metal-rimmed spectacles. He ambles through the wilderness of psychiatry with amiable innocence. His case workups are incredible melanges of irrelevant, inadequate data. He grabs one fact about the patient, usually an unimportant one, and dictates two pages about it. A diagnosis is appended to the end and some treatment is applied. The lucky patients get treatments that are related to their needs.

Dr. Franklin's correspondence and records are in such a state of chaos that they are proverbial. I once called him for a report on a patient, and three weeks later he telephoned me and started a long, rambling discourse on material that had little or no bearing on the patient's difficulties. I finally had to cut him off. Two months later, at a staff meeting at Elmdale, he inquired how the patient was doing and started off again on his reminiscences about the patient.

Often he cannot find his records at all. There is one story regarding a doctor who called him about a patient and two weeks later got a call that they had finally found the patient's chart in Dr. Franklin's "six months old urgent file." I assure the incredulous reader that these are the actual words used.

Dr. Franklin is an eminently good-natured man, and it is difficult to get angry at him. He is apologetic about his lateness on everything and chats in a pleasant way about his daughter, who teaches at Radcliffe, and his son, who is a plastic surgeon in Omaha. How he ever produced two seemingly intelligent, successful children is one of those anomalies that one encounters in life occasionally.

Dr. Franklin has one piece of scientific knowledge. He got it about twenty-five years ago and, having grabbed it, has never let it go. It is the Funkenstein Test. It is sheer nonsense, but Dr. Franklin is devoted to it and does it on all his patients. It involves the injection of a small amount of adrenalin into the patient and the subsequent recording at five-minute intervals of his blood pressure for half an hour. A curve is then drawn that indicates by its height and shape whether or not the patient will benefit from electroshock treatment. I once met Dr. Franklin at a psychiatric convention. After courteously inquiring about my wife and children, he asked me if I knew that the next day someone was going to read a fifteen-minute paper on the Funkenstein Test. I said I had not known. He urged me to attend that session.

The other full-time member at Elmdale is Dr. Foster, who was reading the minutes of the last meeting when I walked in. He is sixty-five and has spent his entire professional career in private psychiatric hospitals; he has been at Elmdale for twenty-five years. He is a squat, broad-faced man who usually wears a vest over his broad abdomen.

In the setting in which he works, Dr. Foster is minimally competent. He gives psychotic patients more or less what they need, does some superficial counseling with persons in situational upsets, and frequently refers neurotic patients for psychotherapy with one of the men in independent private practice in town. He is fairly popular with many older physicians in Kansas City.

Dr. Foster is a bachelor and lives in a large apartment on

the top floor of the hospital; he and Dr. Singer therefore are usually available for nighttime emergencies and admissions. Dr. Foster occasionally refers obscurely to the women he meets on his vacations at old resort centers on the Gulf Coast, and he winks and smiles as he mentions them. However, every once in a while one of the young male patients in Elmdale complains to his physician that a short, fat doctor came to his room at night and played with his penis. If the attending physician talks to Herb Monroe, Herb says, "I'll have to talk to Foster about that." He never does. Where would he find someone to replace Dr. Foster for the relatively modest salary he receives?

Thus staffed by this interesting crew, and with Herb Monroe firmly at the helm, the good ship Elmdale plies its steady course, year in and year out.

There is one final reason why Elmdale has survived into the 1970's. In the late 1940's Herb and his father saw the writing on the wall, and none of the other middle-aged and elderly proprietors of private psychiatric hospitals was over. They therefore went through a lot of legal hocus-pocus and transformed Elmdale into a nonprofit, nonsectarian, private psychiatric hospital under a lay board of directors. The Monroes deeded the hospital buildings, grounds, and equipment to this new directorate without compensation. The nobleness of this act was somewhat dimmed by the fact that five of the board of directors were members of the Monroe family and two others were old friends who could be counted on to vote with them. Then the new hospital hired Herb's father as administrator, Herb as clinical director, and Herb's wife as administrative assistant, all at handsome salaries. The other full-time staff members were continued at their usual stipends, and Elmdale barged on as a tax-free philanthropic institution.

There is, however, a cloud on Elmdale's horizon. Herb is

224

in his middle sixties now, and none of his children or their spouses is a physician. When he dies, the Monroe family, for the first time since the hospital was founded, will not have a physician on its staff, and it is doubtful that they will have either the capacity or the interest to carry on. Whether Elmdale will in fact then become a nonprofit philanthropic hospital or will slowly decay and eventually close is in question. My guess is that without Herb's political shrewdness and showmanship it will close within ten years after his death. The building is already dilapidated, and its grounds are in a district where real estate values are low. There will be no spoils.

The meetings at Elmdale usually last until 10:30 or 11:00. Somebody is always trying to change something. The younger psychiatrists attempt to improve the place, and this precipitates long discussions. They would like better nurses and aides to be hired, expansion of the occupational-therapy department, improvement of the activities program for the patients, and a hundred other things. Three or four times a year some exasperated doctor even makes a motion that they repaint the wards, since visitors complain about the paint flakes peeling off the walls.

Herb has a faultless manner for handling reformers. After a motion is made and seconded to do something or other to improve the hospital, it must be discussed, and since the chairman is always an underling of Herb's, the discussions can go on until midnight if necessary. Herb gets up and talks at great length about everything except the matter at hand. Dr. Foster then takes over with a long speech of reminiscences of his many years of work in the hospital. The doctors one by one drift out to the parking lot and go home. By the time the matter comes to a vote at 10:30 or 11:00 Herb and his cronies have a majority, and the measure is either tabled or referred to a committee or voted down. In the twenty years during which I have been attending these meetings Herb has lost only one vote; I think it took him a month to get over it.

As the meeting drones on, my gaze wanders over the group. There are about half a dozen parapsychiatric professionals here tonight; that is the current jargon term for clinical psychologists, psychiatric social workers, psychiatric nurses, mental-health-service administrators, and other nonphysician mental-health professional workers. Herb Monroe is careful to make many of the parapsychiatric professionals "affiliate members" of Elmdale; as such, they can attend meetings, but cannot vote. Also, under the actual or alleged supervision of a psychiatrist on the Elmdale staff, the clinical psychologists and others of them who are in private practice can send their patients who become severely depressed or otherwise very disturbed to Elmdale and can continue to see them throughout their hospital stays. At the Elmdale meetings the parapsychiatric professionals meet a lot of psychiatrists whom they otherwise would rarely see, and they pick up referrals for psychological testing, psychotherapy (especially of children and adolescents), and other services. Moreover, three times a year Herb Monroe finds the money to invite a distinguished psychiatrist from the East or West Coast to Elmdale for a five-day series of lectures, seminars, and case presentations, and these are useful sessions for the parapsychiatric professionals to attend. These seminars, incidentally, are advertised to the medical profession in general over a twenty-county area, and any interested physician may attend. Although only a sprinkling of out-of-town physicians come, it allows Herb to send notices to every physician in the Kansas City catchment area three times a year and thus keep Elmdale's name fresh

226

in their memories; this is known as "ethical advertising."

The parapsychiatric professionals, like all other groups, are a mixed bag.

Nick Bosworth, who is sitting a couple of tables away from me, is an able clinical psychologist who does better work with rebellious adolescents than most of the psychiatrists in town. He has a knack for getting close to them, and his command of adolescent jargon is faultless. Of course, he is to some extent a forty-year-old rebellious adolescent himself. Rarely is a radical political or social cause so wild or so hopeless that it does not engage his fervent support. On numerous occasions he has risen at Elmdale meetings to say things that are harmful to physicians' blood pressures. Herb Monroe has talked to him about it several times: "We've all got to give a little and take a little. We must see the other fellow's point of view, since we all have to live under one roof. We must close ranks and form a united front. There's always more than one side to a story." Herb can pack more clichés into one minute than any man I know; it's an art.

Norbert Winthrop, a black psychologist, is sagely puffing his pipe and paying close attention to the speakers. He is pleasant, but maintains his dignity to the point of being a little stuffy. He doffs his suit coat only when it is unbearably hot, and his suits and neckties are conservative in cut and color. He does careful psychological testing and his reports are meticulously written. Winthrop knows that as a clinical psychologist in private pactice, he is breaking new ground for a black man in Kansas City, and he is making sure that he doesn't stumble.

Martha Wilson, a PhD psychiatric nurse who teaches in two nursing schools, is sitting at a table with three psychiatrists near the front. She is an attractive, shrewd woman in her early forties. She is physically trim; she rides a bicycle twice around Loose Park every morning. There is something sexy about a good-looking woman riding a bicycle. I guess it's the way she straddles the seat and her legs pump up and down. Once, while watching a teenage girl with long blond hair riding a bicycle, I rammed my car into the back end of a delivery truck. No serious damage was done to anything but my ego. On that day I realized that I was middle-aged and that the best years of my life were over. Martha skillfully wards off the passes that married psychiatrists make at her. With the unmarried ones she's more flexible. She's been married a couple of times, but is single just now. Professionally, she knows what she's doing.

And so the list goes on. I see the Rev. Dr. Andrews sitting on the other side of the room. He is a black-maned, handsome man in his fifties, with a noble profile and a manner that inspires confidence. He was the pastor of a large Presbyterian congregation for twenty years, but left it to go into counseling on what amounts to a private-practice basis. He has an elaborate set of offices in downtown Kansas City. A picture of Christ healing the sick hangs over an expensive leather sofa in the waiting room, and soft religious music purrs to the waiting counselees to put them in a proper frame of mind. He specializes in marriage guidance, but dabbles in many other kinds of problems.

During the final years of his pastorate the Rev. Dr. Andrews took courses in psychology at various Kansas City colleges and universities and flew here and there over the nation to attend one-week seminars on psychotherapy. He has written three books with titles that run something like *Christ Is the Counselor, Christian Psychotherapy,* and *One Way, One Answer.* They are published by a prominent New York house and sell fairly well at religious book stores from coast to coast. The Rev. Dr. Andrews' picture is on a gloss page facing the title page of each of his books. He has been on national television talk shows a few times.

But I fear that the Rev. Dr. Andrews is made of flesh no purer than the rest of us and that when he prays for forgiveness of his sins, he has something to dig his teeth into. I imagine that Mrs. Turner provided material for at least one tête-à-tête between the Rev. Dr. Andrews and his Maker.

The Turners were referred to me by their family physician, who personally called to make the appointment. "They have a kooky story," he said, "and she's all upset. She cries a lot."

"What kind of kooky story?" I asked.

"They'll tell you."

Mr. and Mrs. Turner came together. Mr. Turner said that he'd like to sit in on the session, and for the first appointment or two I often agree to such requests. At this stage the patients know more about their problems than I do.

While Mr. Turner, a plump man in his middle thirties, fidgeted, stared at his hands, and glanced up at me occasionally, his wife told me in a rambling way about her minor phobias, her occasional anxiousness, and the fact that she had never achieved orgasm. She said that often she was irritable with her three children and that she cried frequently and didn't know why. She stated that she had a good husband and a sound family life, but didn't find her home and her church work enough.

I listened to her in silence for about fifteen minutes, waiting for the "kooky story" to come out.

Finally her husband broke in.

"Doctor, in psychiatry, do you have something called the 'father-daughter trick'?"

I indicated that I had never heard that expression, but that, in explaining psychiatric concepts to patients, some psychiatrists had special terms for putting complicated things into simple phrases.

"Yes, but do you have this thing called the 'father-daughter trick'?" he repeated.

I said that I thought the word "trick" was unfortunate in any psychiatric context and that we had no tricks. As to the "father-daughter trick," I couldn't connect it with anything specific and asked him if he could explain it to me.

He glanced at his wife, and then he looked around the room for a minute. After that he told me their "kooky story" while his wife stared at the floor.

About six months previous to that time, his wife had gone to the pastor of her church to talk about her fears, her tenseness, and her vague dissatisfactions. He said that he didn't have much talent at counseling unless it dealt with strictly religious matters and referred her to the Rev. Dr. Andrews. He told her about the three books the Rev. Dr. Andrews had written and said he was a nationally known man. She consulted him. In the third session he told her that he felt that her case required the technique known in psychiatry as the "father-daughter trick."

To make an ugly story brief, the "father-daughter trick" consisted of having sexual intercourse with Mrs. Turner once or twice a week for three months on a couch in his office. With the black-maned, noble-profiled Rev. Dr. Andrews, Mrs. Turner had orgasms on a few occasions.

Then her guilt got the best of her and she stopped going to see him. He called her once to invite her to continue "the treatment," and she made an appointment, but did not keep it. The Rev. Dr. Andrews called no more, and a couple of months went by. Finally her guilt became intolerable, and she broke down and told her husband. He didn't know

230

what to make of it. He was a sheet-metal worker; to him psychiatry was a mysterious thing, and the Rev. Dr. Andrews was a minor god in the Presbyterian pantheon. The Rev. Dr. Andrews had preached a time or two, as guest preacher, at their church and had made a strong impression. At first Mr. Turner thought that his wife was "making it up" for some reason or that she had developed delusions. But she wasn't the kind who "made things up," and she didn't seem delusional.

Moreover, there was the uncomfortable problem that if this story was true, this "treatment" could not have gone on for three months without the willing consent of his wife. She was not a stupid woman, and if these things had actually occurred, the Rev. Dr. Andrews was not the only one who had broken the seventh commandment.

Three weeks went by, during which both Mr. and Mrs. Turner were increasingly miserable. She cried a lot, and her phobias and anxiety grew worse. Then Mr. Turner dragged her, quite reluctantly, to see their family doctor. He didn't know what to do and suggested that the only way to get at the truth was for them to go together to talk to the Rev. Dr. Andrews. So they went to his office to make an appointment, but that week the Rev. Dr. Andrews was in Michigan giving a series of lectures and seminars on pastoral counseling at a seminary. The receptionist said that he would be back in the office on the following Monday.

They went back on the following Monday. Between patients, the receptionist buzzed the Rev. Dr. Andrews, told him that the Turners were there, and listened while he spoke briefly to her on the intercom. She then told the Turners that the Rev. Dr. Andrews was booked up, that he could take on no new patients at that time, even if they were persons he had formerly treated, and recommended that they see the Rev. Mr. Wallman, who did counseling in the same section of the city in which they lived. The receptionist said that Mr. Wallman was an excellent therapist who had had part of his training under the Rev. Dr. Andrews.

"Tell him we'll see him if we have to wait here all day," Mr. Turner said, "and we'll be right here in the waiting room when he leaves, if he won't see us any other time."

The receptionist went into the Rev. Dr. Andrews' office. After a moment she came out and said that since Mrs. Turner was a former patient, the Rev. Dr. Andrews had consented to see them briefly, if they would wait. They waited, and an hour later they were ushered in.

The Rev. Dr. Andrews greeted them with effusive solemnity and talked steadily for thirty minutes. He mentioned his vast experience in treating emotionally upset people and told them at length about his three books, which were used in pastoral counseling courses all over the country. He spoke of his heavy commitments in therapy and teaching as he trod the path on which Christ had set his feet. He emphasized his dedication to his patients, his sacrifices in working to help them, and the arduousness of his tasks.

He talked solemnly and compassionately, and without bitterness, about how some patients misunderstood, or misinterpreted, or, in their confused mental states, said things about the therapy that were not so, which was not dishonesty on their part, but a product of their mental difficulties and often a sign that they had lost the vital contact with Christ that was so crucial in the lives of us all, but that they were not to be blamed for that, since they were confused and ill. And how even he, the Rev. Dr. Andrews, had been accused of the most outlandish things, but which everyone knew could not be true, and how deeply such things affected him, but that each person had to take up the cross Christ gave him and wear the crown of thorns required of him. And that he, the Rev. Dr. Andrews, accepted the cruel things that an occasional patient might say; it was a cross he had to bear, a crown of thorns he had to endure, a thorn in his flesh he had to suffer as he labored to relieve mental suffering. However, he would not be deterred, never, from the work Christ had set him to do by false rumors, or scandalous accusations, or any other trials God put him to, and that he hoped Mrs. Turner was doing better after his counseling with her, and he knew she was, though, of course, she would have her ups and downs, and life was not easy, nor had Christ meant it to be so, for if He meant it to be otherwise He would not have died on the cross for us. He was sure that in the long run, if not in the short run, Mrs. Turner would be better, and that often the fruit took time to ripen on the bough, and that some sowed for others to reap, and that seed cast upon the ground grew and bloomed in its own time, according to God's laws. So it was with Christian counseling, for often the benefits matured with time, long after the actual treatment was terminated.

However, he could not see her more right now because of the many calls upon his time, both in Kansas City and in other places all over the nation. Next week he had to go to Lexington, Kentucky, to give a ten-day course on pastoral counseling, and he had just come back from a similar trip to Michigan, and the Rev. Mr. Wallman could carry on with Mrs. Turner the work that had been started with him, for Mr. Wallman had studied with him and was thoroughly adept in Christian counseling. Moreover, the Rev. Mr. Wallman's office was in the same section of town in which the Turners lived. And the Rev. Dr. Andrews filled thirty minutes with all this, and much more, and the Turners did

233

not have an opportunity to ask a single question, and then, speaking continually, he talked them to the door, talked them into the waiting room and out into the corridor, and smiling benignly, shook hands with them both and retired, closing the door to the waiting room behind him.

Mr. Turner, cowed and puzzled by all this, drove home with his wife in silence, but after thinking it over for a couple of hours, decided that the Rev. Dr. Andrews was a son of a bitch.

So they sat there before me, their marriage destroyed but held together by three small children. She was more upset than ever, and he had begun to drink too much. I lamely suggested that she might enter psychotherapy with me, but after one unhappy experience with it Mr. Turner was obviously skeptical. They said they'd think it over. I never heard from them again.

People who ought to know better sometimes recommend psychotherapy on the grounds that it can do no harm and may do some good. Unfortunately I've seen a fair number of Mrs. Turners, though the techniques by which they were damaged usually were more subtle than that used by the Rev. Dr. Andrews.

I've been at Elmdale for twenty minutes. I've signed the attendance roll. A hubbub starts up over something. I am sitting near the door and at an opportune moment, when the others are distracted by whatever is going on, I slip into the corridor.

As I go through the lobby, I notice my name written in chalk on the blackboard that is propped up near the main door on staff-meeting nights. The names of three other doctors are on the board, with telephone numbers after them. After my name is scribbled, "Call Lutheran ER."

I go to the nearby switchboard, nod to the girl on duty, and look up the number of the Lutheran United Hospital on the list of commonly called numbers on a large sheet under the glass cover of the switchboard girl's desk. I dial the number, ask for the emergency room, and identify myself. Someone, probably an aide, asks me to hold the line for a minute. I wait for two minutes, and just as I am debating whether to hang up and go on, Mark Schriefer picks up the phone and greets me.

"Harry, where are you?"

"I'm just leaving Elmdale. There's a staff meeting going on, but I'm ducking out early."

"Drop by the emergency room of Lutheran as you drive home," he says. "It's only a few blocks out of your way. We need your signature for something."

"What kind of something?"

"Al Bromley is dead. He took a shoeboxful of tranquilizers. There's no doubt that it's suicide. He left a note. The men from the coroner's office are here. I know you took care of Al once or twice. You can verify that he was . . . well, you know . . . and can sign the emergency-room sheet and the coroner's report. That will satisfy the coroner's office and then they'll release the body to the undertaker."

"I'm sorry to hear this," I say. "I'll be there in fifteen minutes."

14

AS I drove to Lutheran United, snow began to fall; I turned on my windshield wipers and went more slowly. As the snow grew thicker, I pulled over to the curb, stopped, and fastened my seat belt. I have no fear of death; in fact, it sometimes looks attractive to me. However, I have too great a sense of responsibility to hurry it along by being imprudent.

Al Bromley was dead.

Another one, but this time it was not one of my patients.

Every psychiatrist has patients he would like to forget; they haunt him from time to time. At the top of the list are his suicides. Homicide by psychiatric patients, though it makes headlines when it occurs, is statistically rare. I've never had a patient who while under my care or after discharge from it committed homicide. Suicide is another matter.

As I drove cautiously through the falling snow, I counted some of the beads on my rosary of suicides and did penance, much against my will.

Miss Dawson, age nineteen, was a student nurse from a small town in southern Ohio who came to study nursing at the medical center in which I took my psychiatric residency. She became depressed and was assigned to be treated by me, under the supervision of Dr. Berry. Dr. Berry was in private practice, but held a clinical associate professorship at the medical school and supervised resident psychiatrists a couple of hours a week in his office. I spent fifty minutes with him once a week to discuss in detail one case that I was treating.

During his supervisory sessions with me Dr. Berry took a small blackboard from a cabinet and set it on a wooden chair. With a piece of chalk he drew on the blackboard the Freudian egg and by two horizontal lines divided it into three equal parts, stacked on top of one another. The top third of the egg was labeled superego, the middle third was ego, and the bottom part was id.

Then the battle began. As I presented the material from my interviews with Miss Dawson, he drew vector arrows from the superego slashing down into the ego; they looked like the arrows of advancing armored divisions in newspaper maps of military battles. Other arrows and small rectangles or squares represented the counterattacking forces and the reserve battalions of the ego. The ego, from a military point of view, had a bad situation, since it also suffered frequent incursions from the id below it. Often it had to fight on two fronts simultaneously. In addition the beleaguered ego was continually skirmishing with "reality": This was designated by still more arrows that horizontally pierced the rim of the egg. Some of these arrows went from the ego, through the eggshell, to the open space outside it; they indicated the ego's approaches to "reality." Still other arrows were directed from the outside space, through the eggshell, into the ego; they indicated "reality's" impact on the ego. In Miss Dawson's case "reality" included her domineering father, her floundering mother, her classmates, the nursing school, me, and other things.

Our task, Dr. Berry explained, was to help the ego

mobilize and deploy its forces in the best possible ways to repel the incursions from the superego and to drive the advancing troops from the id back into their own territory. When the superego forces won a battle over the ego, Miss Dawson felt something that we called guilt, and when the id battalions advanced too far into the ego, Miss Dawson had something else that we called anxiety.

At Yale I had been taught that reasoning by metaphors was an unsound way to discuss scientific problems. I had uneasy doubts about all these military metaphors, and I wondered how much relevance they had to Miss Dawson and her depression. Finally I one day asked Dr. Berry if he really thought that the id, the ego, and the superego existed in patients or if they were merely convenient, somewhat treacherous fictions that we were using to talk more easily about Miss Dawson. He stared at me in silence. I had been in psychiatry for only nine months and I was somewhat naïve, a quality that I have, perhaps at some cost to my happiness, lost since then.

I thought that his silence indicated that he was sagely considering my inquiry, and so I went on to ask if he thought that Freud had actually discovered the id, the ego, and the superego or had merely *invented* them as useful metaphorical devices in discussing psychiatric problems. Since Dr. Berry said nothing, but only continued to stare at me, I went on to say that so far in my reading of Freud it was not clear whether he realized that such things as the ego and the id were only semantic devices; indeed, it appeared that he thought they were natural phenomena rather than artificial contrivances that merely made discussion of emotional difficulties easier. I suggested that things like the ego and superego did not really exist in patients' minds, but only in psychiatrists' minds when they thought about patients. I felt I had put the matter rather nicely and was well pleased with myself.

238

Dr. Berry was furious. He said that these things were the basis of all modern psychiatry, and that they existed just as much as grass and trees existed, and that my use of the word "invent" in referring to Freud showed my utter failure to grasp everything he had been trying to teach me for three months.

Then he got control of himself and lit into me with cold, measured stabs. He stated that for some time he had noted my inability to grasp psychiatric principles. This inability, he said, was caused by my unconscious emotional problems. These problems were preventing me from understanding the emotional turmoil of patients. He added that I was using the ego defenses of intellectualizing and rationalization to protect myself from painful problems within me and that until these unresolved difficulties were solved in thorough psychoanalysis I would be crippled as a therapist.

His punches floored me. I got up, badly battered, but intact. I was aware that he had not dealt with my questions, but had resorted to a frontal personal attack on me. After a brief pause I decided to follow the cowardly dictum that states that he who fights and runs away will live to fight another day. I made weak excuses, pleaded ignorance, cited my youth and inexperience, retracted my questions, and appeased him. As to the psychoanalytic treatment, I said I couldn't afford it just then.

Four days later Miss Dawson took several bottles of sedatives from the medication cabinet of a medical ward, went to her room, and swallowed all the pills. For thirty-six hours I wandered in and out of her hospital room while the medical staff tried to save her. I had to face her parents when they came from Ohio to get the body.

I was a wreck when I went for my next session with Dr. Berry, and when I told him what had happened in the intervening week, he was plainly triumphant. He had no compassion for me, let alone Miss Dawson. He said that he had warned me about my inability to grasp patients' difficulties because of my unconscious, unresolved problems. He drew the Freudian egg on the blackboard as I gloomily watched, and he showed me how the invading columns from the superego had grown stronger, producing marked guilt in Miss Dawson, and how the onslaughts from the id had further eroded her crumbling ego strength. A weak arrow directed inward from outside the eggshell indicated my lack of support for her disintegrating ego. This inadequate support from the therapist, he said, had caused total collapse of her ego structure and had produced her suicide.

I never objected to or questioned anything Dr. Berry said during the three further months in which I had supervisory sessions with him, but that day I concluded he was one of the most brutal bastards I had ever known.

My rosary of suicides has other nail-studded beads. One of them is for Miss Long, age seventy-two, a successful businesswoman who after forty years with her company was forced by its rules to retire. She went to live with relatives in California, but felt desolate there and returned to live in a large apartment in central Kansas City. She tried to get interested in civic work, philanthropic organizations, and church groups, but none of it held her interest.

She ground on for four more years. Then she began to have trouble remembering where she put her purse, and where her checkbook was, and what the names of her neighbors in the apartment building were. She realized that she was becoming senile. She went to her family physician with the complaint of insomnia and bought the sleeping pills he prescribed. She wrote a brief letter stating why she was terminating her life, and in it she gave the name and address of the lawyer who had her will. She then took all the sleeping pills and went to bed. Two days later the apartment-building manager, with the police, unlocked the door of her apartment and found her lying in a stupor. She did not die.

She was psychiatrically hospitalized under my care; it was during the second year of my private practice. After four weeks on the Mt. Sinai psychiatric ward she was cheerful and active, and in a gracious way she told me that she had done a foolish thing and would never do it again. She cajoled me into transferring her to a general medical service on the third floor of the hospital. Two hours after settling into her new room she dressed in her street clothes, walked up to the fifth floor, and threw herself from a window into the doctors' parking lot below.

I sat in the administrator's office at Mt. Sinai and explained it all to the administrator and an agent from the county coroner's office, and then I read about it that evening in the Kansas City *Star*; the article had a photograph of the side of the hospital from which she had jumped, with a white arrow that went from the window out of which she had leaped to the pavement of the parking lot. I also had to explain her death to her relatives who came from California for the funeral and the reading of the will. The bank that was the executor of her estate called me three months later and requested that I send my bill to them so that the residue of the estate could be precisely stated; I did so, and two weeks later the bank sent me a check. It was several years before I ceased to remember Miss Long momentarily every time I parked my car in the Mt. Sinai doctors' parking lot.

There are more beads to count as I say my reluctant penance. There were Mr. McDonald, age twenty-six, who leaped from the observation car of a speeding railroad train, and Mrs. Bonelli, who took four bottles of antidepressant pills that I had prescribed for her and that she had patiently accumulated. Mr. Daniels hanged himself in his basement;

241

his wife found him when she went down to put some dirty clothes in the washing machine. Maxine Warner leaped from a dormitory window at college after writing me a long farewell letter; I received it eighteen hours after she died. Mr. Howard parked his car on a deserted dirt road on a bright spring morning; he ran a garden hose from the exhaust pipe to a narrowly opened window of the front seat and patiently waited for death as his motor ran. There are others.

I haven't had any suicides during the past three years and only one in the last five years. It's not because I've grown wiser, but because I avoid risky cases, like the wrist slasher I sent to Terry Jackson today. As I grow older and my own death draws nearer, I become too painfully anxious and depressed when a patient destroys himself because I didn't pick up the right cues, or was careless, or erred in my judgment, or, perhaps, had bad luck.

At a little past 8:00 I entered the emergency room of Luteran United Hospital. Until the First World War it was the German Hospital of Kansas City, but in 1918 they changed the name. One year earlier, and for similar reasons, the British royal family changed its name from Saxe-Coburg-Gotha to Windsor.

However, the names of the members of the board of directors of Lutheran United, even into the 1970's, are still predominantly German; they and many of its leading physicians are descendants of the Germans who flooded into Missouri and Kansas between 1850 and 1880 when Prussian militarism began to dominate Germany. President Eisenhower, who spent his childhood and adolescence in a small Kansas town near Kansas City, had a brother who died in Lutheran United, and Mark Schriefer is also of old Kansas City German stock.

In the emergency room bright light glared from one

white, tiled wall to another, and there was the unique medicinal smell, probably of Merthiolate and other antiseptic drugs, that emergency rooms everywhere exude.

I looked around. I rarely go to Lutheran United and I didn't know anyone in the room. The girl at the receptionist's desk looked up at me carelessly and then went on filling out a form. I went to her and said I was Dr. Chapman and that Dr. Schriefer had put in a call for me.

She didn't grasp what I wanted. I added that it concerned a Dr. Bromley who apparently had been brought in dead or had died there during the last hour or so.

"Oh, the suicide," she said and nodded toward a set of double, swinging metal doors to her left. "In there."

I went through the door and saw Mark Schriefer talking with an obese man in a heavy coat and a dirty felt hat. An unshaven, lean man of fifty was beside him. All three were seated on metal stools. A sheet covered and outlined a body on the examining table in the center of the room.

Mark got up, thanked me for coming, and presented me to the two other men.

"These are the men from the coroner's office," he said, turning to them. "Excuse me, I forgot your names."

"Barkley," said the obese man, "Sam Barkley."

"Johnson," said the other, apparently his assistant or his driver.

Mark took over. "Harry, we just need to verify that Al had certain kinds of psychiatric problems and that there is no good reason to feel that this is anything but suicide. His wife and his mother are, of course, pretty upset. So I thought it would be easier for you to give Mr. Barkley the facts than to drag his family through this. We must satisfy Mr. Barkley that this is a clear-cut suicide, so that the body can be released to the undertaker."

I felt that it would not be too hard to convince Mr. Barkley. It was a routine case for him, and although it

243

would perhaps be unjust to assume that he was a political ward heeler who had been made a coroner's deputy for delivering his precinct in the last election, he certainly looked the picture of such a public servant.

Mr. Barkley shoved a piece of paper at me and said, "He left this."

I looked at the paper. It was a prescription-pad sheet with "Alfred J. Bromley, MD" printed at the top; an office address and telephone number were under his name. It was an office he had opened briefly and had then closed several years previously.

A short message was scrawled on the sheet. "I'm calling it quits. I have no life insurance. This note will clarify the situation for whoever finds me. My wife, kids, and everybody else will be better off this way. I'm sorry. Alfred J. Bromley." Doctors' suicide notes are usually brief and to the point; they know the facts that have to be covered. I've seen three or four such notes.

I handed it back to the coroner's deputy.

"It's pretty obvious," I said.

"You treated him, did you?" Mr. Barkley asked.

"Not exactly," I replied. "But I know all about him. He was a narcotic addict. He's been hospitalized several times in Kansas City to be taken off the stuff. I did it twice at Mt. Sinai. He always signed out against medical advice a week or so after withdrawal from the drug. Other psychiatrists have withdrawn him at other hospitals in town. This has been going on for about ten years; it started when he was twenty-five or so. The narcotic agents know him. They took away his narcotic license years ago, and they've forced him to go to Fort Worth for treatment a couple of times. You know the story."

"Was he practicing?" Mr. Barkley asked.

"He worked on and off," I said. "He's worked for Dr. Monroe at Elmdale several times, but only for a few months

244

each time. When he went back on narcotics, or at least when he was so badly on them that it was obvious, they'd discharge him. He's worked covering the emergency rooms in small hospitals that don't have interns. He's also worked for short periods in the accident sections at the Ford plant, TWA, and other industrial setups. But it was always the same story. It never lasted long. He made one or two attempts at private practice, but failed. I don't think he's worked much lately."

"General doctor, then," Mr. Barkley said.

That was the point that hurt most.

"Originally," I said, "he was a psychiatrist, a fully trained, board-certified psychiatrist who took his training at one of the best centers in New York. He had a couple of years of analysis in New York; he didn't finish it. However, for the last three or four years he's done any kind of work he could."

"A shrink who couldn't cure himself," said Mr. Barkley, and he laughed.

I suppose that a man who makes his living looking at dead bodies soon loses compassion for the merchandise he deals in. However, I doubted that Mr. Barkley had much compassion to begin with.

"Well, that's good enough for me," Mr. Barkley added. "Another junkie who ran out of stuff and couldn't face coming off it cold turkey. Sign here, Doctor."

He handed me a smudged form onto which the girl in the outside office had typed the relevant data.

I signed where he pointed after glancing over the sheet quickly. I've seen my share of them and I know what to check.

"Two carbons," he said.

I signed the two carbons.

"Well, gentlemen, that's it." He took a pad of printed forms from his suit coat pocket and wrote a few words in various blank spaces on it. He signed it and passed it with a ballpoint pen to his assistant to sign.

"There," he said, handing the paper to Mark, "that releases the body."

He rose, adjusted his hat, and began to button his heavy coat.

"Cold," he said. "Cold for March. In like a lion, out like a lamb."

He shook our hands heartily. "Sam Barkley," he said. "I don't think either of you gentlemen lives in my district, but anytime I can do anything for you, just let me know." His associate nodded in a friendly way, and they went out.

Mark gave me a couple of emergency-room forms to sign, and I did so.

I went to the table and uncovered Al Bromley's head. His body already had the smell of decaying flesh, and his leaden lips were slightly apart. His face was pale and thin and had two or three days' growth of stubble on it; he looked much older than he was, and there were many gray hairs among the black ones on his cheeks, jaw, and upper lip.

"Sometimes I think we're a sick profession," I said.

"Probably no sicker than the others," Mark answered. "We just know more doctors, since we have to live with them."

"Maybe so," I said, "but a couple of years ago I totaled up the number of hours in a month that I spent taking care of physicians, their wives, and their adolescent children, and it came to about twenty-five percent. It's been less lately."

"That's just the nature of your practice," Mark said.

"Not entirely," I replied.

Al Bromley's face both fascinated and saddened me as I looked at it.

"Someday," I said, musing, "I'm going to write a book

246

titled *The Psychopathology of Kansas City Physicians and Their Families.* I have plenty of case material in my files. It will be published posthumously."

We laughed. Nervous laughter.

I rambled on. "The number of doctors who become narcotic addicts and are lost to the profession is equal to the total graduating class of one medical school every year. When I was in military service, I spent a year and a half at the Public Health Service Hospital in Fort Worth. We always had three hundred narcotic addicts there in one section, and six hundred general psychiatric patients from the Coast Guard, the Navy, and the Merchant Marine. For nine hundred patients we had about twenty psychiatrists, but only one general physician. Do you know why we needed only one general physician for all those patients?"

Mark shook his head.

"Because we always had at least half a dozen physician addict patients who were well qualified professionally, and we simply put them to work running the sick bay, covering the morning sick call, taking care of injured hospital employees, and doing all the routine physical exams and checkups. We had board-certified surgeons, internists, dermatologists, and other kinds of specialists. They did everything except get near the narcotics; only the one staff general physician was allowed to dispense them. Pretty sad, isn't it?"

"Yeah," Mark said.

I turned my gaze away from Al Bromley's face. "On top of that, we always had half a dozen old, burned-out junkie physicians who weren't fit to do medical work. They just floated around the place. The narcotic agents don't like to prosecute a doctor. They tell him it's four months at a hospital or prosecution, and he goes to Fort Worth or Lexington or somewhere else."

Something about Al Bromley held me. I passed my hand

247

over his cold, hard lips and cheek. Maybe it was because I had known some relatives of his; most of his family lived in Kansas City.

"His father was a doctor, you know," I said. "He gave my mother an anesthesia many years ago. He died shortly after Al graduated from med school. I doubt Al saw his father much while he was growing up. Just another fatherless, husbandless doctor's family—while Daddy is out saving lives."

"You're in a bitter mood tonight," Mark said, but he didn't argue with me.

"The irony of the whole damned business," I went on, "is that the average American doctor works most of the time to pay for his overhead and taxes. I once told the dean over at the med school that they teach their students how to treat patients but they don't teach them how to practice medicine and lead sensible lives while doing so. I told him they ought to give the students courses on how to adjust to being doctors."

"And what did he say?"

"He said, 'Who'd teach such a course?' And I told him that I would. He didn't like that. He considered himself the one and only expert on all things medical. He just walked away."

"Which dean was that?" Mark asked.

"Beardsley," I replied.

"He was a horse's ass," Mark said.

"I know, but the laymen think he's great. He's now on the President's Council for Medical Education and seventeen other national committees. I think he spends half his life on airplanes going to and from committee meetings. And the bastard has never practiced medicine. The average aide in an emergency room knows more about what actually goes on in medical practice than he does."

We were silent for a minute or so.

248

Three doctors, two of us alive.

"That's the second physician suicide I've seen since Christmas," Mark said. "I wasn't Al's doctor. I guess nobody was. But I take care of his wife and kids. So when they found him, they called me."

"Where did they find him?" I asked.

"In a room at the downtown YMCA. His wife says she last saw him on Saturday morning. It's an awful way for a doctor to go."

"Yeah, but a lot of them do," I said. "Suicide is the eleventh most common cause of death in the general population, but the fifth most common cause of death among doctors. The crusher is that it's the fourth most common cause of death among psychiatrists. I'd have to use all the fingers of both hands to count the number of psychiatrists whom I personally have known who ended this way."

"Why?"

"Why?" I repeated. "Who knows why? Maybe because we see so much of it that we get accustomed to it, and it comes easily when the debits in life get bigger than the credits. Maybe it's because we're sicker than the others when we go into this line in the first place. Perhaps we're looking for answers, and maybe some of us don't find them. Or perhaps we just do it in ways that are more obvious, and that raises the totals on death certificates and statistics. Who knows why about anything?"

We stood in uncomfortable silence.

I covered Al Bromley's head.

I put my hand on Mark's shoulder, facing him.

"There's one other possible answer," I said.

"What's that?"

"Maybe we know something the rest of you don't know."

He gave a snorting laugh.

I shook his shoulder in a friendly way, turned, and left.

15

AT a little after 9:00 I arrive home. I kiss my wife and look in at my two late-adolescent boys studying in their rooms. The older of them is a top student, pleasant but quiet. He probably will go into one of the professions; he says it will be engineering, but sometimes he talks about medicine. I have to shake the younger one by the shoulder to get his attention; he studies with headphones on, attached to a stereo set playing rock-music cassettes. He is clever with anything mechanical and probably will end up a gregarious, rambunctious businessman. I also have a girl in medical school in Chicago; she is a savvy, well-self-controlled rebel. I sit and talk with each of my boys for a few minutes and then go back to my wife in the family room. She turns off the TV.

"How did it go today?" she asks.

I tell her about Al Bromley's death. I don't want to talk about it, and by wordless agreement, we drop the subject after a few sentences.

"The only other big news is from the St. Catharine's departmental meeting." I tell her in detail how the Infernal Quartet were overthrown and cast into outer darkness. She smiles and agrees that it will be a good thing for the psychiatric ward at St. Catharine's.

"But they still control the psychiatric section of Bethesda," she says.

"In time it will go the same way as St. Catharine's," I answer. "Slowly, more psychiatrists will be voted onto the psychiatric staff at general staff meetings. Then they'll begin to squabble over beds, and one night the new men will do what was done at St. Catharine's tonight."

"When they cut their beds down at Bethesda, Arthur Downs will probably perforate his ulcer and Larry Packard will drink himself into the DT's," my wife says.

"Perhaps," I reply, "Arthur is really a scared little boy underneath all the geniality and bluster. He almost trembled as he left St. Catharine's tonight."

We talk about the children, some furniture my wife is thinking of buying, a dinner engagement we have on Thursday, and other things.

"Oh," my wife says, "your mother brought over a cardboard box. It's there on the table. She said she was cleaning out a closet, and before throwing out all that old stuff, she wanted you to look it over. She said to throw away what you don't want and to keep the rest."

My mother lives about a ten-minute drive from us. She lives alone with a poodle dog in the same house in which I was reared; she's lived in it for slightly more than half a century. She drives a car and handles her own business affairs. When boys come to her door to shovel the snow, she offers them twenty-five cents, bawls them out when they ask for three dollars, and does it herself. She finds it outrageous that people want to make more money than they did in the 1930's. She left the Methodist church when they started discussing sociology in the pulpit and now attends the First Church of Christ the Nazarene, where they discuss more important subjects like heaven and hell.

My mother is made of stern, hard stuff. She was reared on a wheat ranch in Canada, and her parents were British farmers who emigrated to Ontario in the 1870's. On winter mornings she broke the ice in the basin in her room to wash

251

her face, and one of the strongest memories of her childhood is the jubilation in her home when the British troops relieved Ladysmith in the Boer War. When my mother was eleven, her father slipped from the top of a wheat combine, and his leg was badly mangled in the blades. He was bleeding to death, and when the doctor came he amputated it at once, without an anesthetic. He didn't scream, but my mother still remembers his groans from behind the closed door of his bedroom during the operation.

In her late teens my mother, the youngest of nine children, left home and took nurses' training in Connecticut. Afterward she became an X-ray nurse in New York City. There she met my father, an ebullient salesman who had been an infantry captain in the First World War and had lost a finger and three ribs in the process. They married and traveled about the country for two years until I was born in 1924 in San Francisco, where my father was setting up a sales organization for a laundry-supply company. When I was born, he took a job in Kansas City in which he wouldn't have to travel.

I go to the table, pick up the large cardboard box, and carry it back to my chair. The box is carefully wrapped in newspapers and neatly tied with heavy string. My mother's touch. If a thing's worth doing, it's worth doing well.

I open it, a Pandora's box of nostalgia. My Boy Scout merit badge sash with thirty-four merit badges neatly sewn on, my Eagle Scout pin, and my high school annuals. Paul Farnsworth, whom I saw today with his addicted son in the St. Catharine's emergency room, is in my high school annuals somewhere. I look him up and see the same face that I saw today, though unmarked with the haggard despair it had this morning. There are a lot of other things in the box.

252

At the bottom is an old scrapbook with a dried leaf pasted on each page, my leaf collection.

It's been thirty-five years or more since I thought about my leaf collection and more than forty years since I pasted the last leaf in it. When I was in grade school, I collected leaves from about one hundred species of the trees in the Kansas City area, pressed them in heavy books, and pasted them in this scrapbook. A few leaves crack and crumble as I turn the pages, and so I turn the pages more carefully.

The television set is on again, but my reminiscences are going back to another world. They return to a somewhat shy boy in corduroy knickers and hand-knit woolen sweaters who pasted leaves in a scrapbook, and to a studious high school student who intended to be a biologist. He was a bright boy, and later he studied biology at Yale.

Then one night in early December, 1941, as I was eating dinner at Yale, a friend rushed to our table and said, "The Japs have bombed Pearl Harbor. Roosevelt's going to give a speech on the radio. We're at war." Two days later I went to the dean's office and changed my major from biology to premed. I foresaw that virtually all my classmates except the premed students would be gone by the following June. Survival is the first rule of life.

So I abandoned the beetles, the spiders, and the algae, and I took up the study of man. In 1943 I entered medical school while the horrid butchery of war was killing 5 percent of my Yale class and maiming many others. Although I did well enough in medical school, it really didn't interest me until I got to psychiatry in the third year. After a week in psychiatry I knew that it would be my specialty. It absorbed me as nothing else in medicine did. Though I have not always been happy in my specialty, I have rarely been bored.

I'm getting tired, but I make it a rule not to go to bed until 10:00. Sometimes I nod off in my chair, and my wife tells me to go to bed. But I never break my rule. My mother's influence, I guess.

It's a few minutes before 10:00.

The telephone rings. Paradise will be a place where there are no telephones.

"Harry?"

"Yes."

"This is Steve Robins." He is a family doctor in North Kansas City.

"What is it, Steve?"

"Sorry to bother you at this time of night."

"That's all right. What's the trouble?"

"I'm on the OB ward at Clay County Memorial. It's a postpartum case. She's about twenty-five or so. I delivered her three days ago. She was fine until this afternoon. Then she started hearing voices and she thinks the FBI is trying to kill her."

"Has she ever been like this before?"

"No. The family are all upset, and the night nursing supervisor is on my neck. She says I can't keep her here and that I have to get her out tonight. She tried to run down the corridor and leave the hospital in her nightgown. I have relatives watching at her bedside now."

"All right. What are her full name and address?"

He puts his hand over the receiver, evidently talking to a nurse, and then gives me the information.

"Okay," I say. "Let me see where I can find a bed. Give me your telephone number and extension number. All right. I'll call you back in fifteen minutes."

I know Mt. Sinai is probably full, since I got the last bed late this afternoon for Ralph Porter's wrist slasher from Independence. Nevertheless, I call to check; sometimes a patient signs out or is discharged late in the day, opening a bed. However, Mt. Sinai is full, with one patient on the waiting list. I call St. Catharine's. They are full but there's no one on the waiting list. I ask if Sister is in the admission office. She just walked in; she's making rounds before retiring for the night. I ask to talk to her.

The sisters, in general, like me. Maybe I can arrange something with her. I give her the basic details in fifteen seconds, ask her to make room for this patient on the psychiatric ward, and promise to discharge Mrs. Spinelli the next morning. Sister says she'll do it. I thank her. I tell her that Dr. Steven Robins will call in ten minutes to give information both to the admission office and the psychiatric ward. The patient will arrive by ambulance accompanied by two relatives who will give more data and sign the admission papers.

I call the psychiatric floor, apologize for the trouble I'm giving them, outline the case briefly, and leave orders for sedation as soon as the patient reaches the floor.

Then I call Steve Robins and give him this information. He is obviously relieved. I ask him to follow up the patient from the obstetric point of view, which is easy, since he is in St. Catharine's every day. I tell him to instruct the relatives to call my office the next morning to make an appointment to see me, or if they prefer, they can wait for me in the small waiting room outside the psychiatric ward at St. Catharine's about 9 the next morning. I make a note to call Marie at 9:30 to inform her about this patient so she'll know who the relatives are if they telephone my office for an appointment.

The relatives probably are leaning over the counter of the nurses' station; I can hear voices in the background.

Steve asks me when I will see the patient. I reply that I will see her tomorrow morning by 9:30 at the latest, and I explain that appropriate orders already have been left with the nurses on duty at the St. Catharine's psychiatric ward. I emphasize to Steve that he must tell the relatives that two of them must accompany the patient in the ambulance to St. Catharine's and that they must go to the admission office there before they leave the hospital. He says he'll make that clear.

It's all arranged.